Memoirs of Casanova Volume IX

Memoirs of Casanova Volume IX

Giacomo Casanova

MINT EDITIONS

Memoirs of Casanova Volume IX was first published in 1902.

This edition published by Mint Editions 2021.

ISBN 9781513281919 | E-ISBN 9781513286938

Published by Mint Editions®

**MINT
EDITIONS**

minteditionbooks.com

Publishing Director: Jennifer Newens
Design & Production: Rachel Lopez Metzger
Project Manager: Micaela Clark
Translated By: Arthur Machen
Typesetting: Westchester Publishing Services

Contents

I

Supper at My Casino With M. M. and M. de Bernis, the French Ambassador—A Proposal from M. M.; I Accept It—Consequences—C. C. is Unfaithful to Me, and I Cannot Complain

I felt highly pleased with the supper-party I had arranged with M——
M——, and I ought to have been happy. Yet I was not so; but whence came the anxiety which was a torment to me? Whence? From my fatal habit of gambling. That passion was rooted in me; to live and to play were to me two identical things, and as I could not hold the bank I would go and punt at the ridotto, where I lost my money morning and night. That state of things made me miserable. Perhaps someone will say to me:

"Why did you play, when there was no need of it, when you were in want of nothing, when you had all the money you could wish to satisfy your fancies?"

That would be a troublesome question if I had not made it a law to tell the truth. Well, then, dear inquisitive reader, if I played with almost the certainty of losing, although no one, perhaps, was more sensible than I was to the losses made in gambling, it is because I had in me the evil spirit of avarice; it is because I loved prodigality, and because my heart bled when I found myself compelled to spend any money that I had not won at the gaming-table. It is an ugly vice, dear reader, I do not deny it. However, all I can say is that, during the four days previous to the supper, I lost all the gold won for me by M—— M——

On the anxiously-expected day I went to my casino, where at the appointed hour M—— M—— came with her friend, whom she introduced to me as soon as he had taken off his mask.

"I had an ardent wish, sir," said M. de Bernis to me, "to renew acquaintance with you, since I heard from madame that we had known each other in Paris."

With these words he looked at me attentively, as people will do when they are trying to recollect a person whom they have lost sight of. I then told him that we had never spoken to one another, and that he had not seen enough of me to recollect my features now.

"I had the honour," I added, "to dine with your excellency at M. de Mocenigo's house, but you talked all the time with Marshal Keith, the Prussian ambassador, and I was not fortunate enough to attract your attention. As you were on the point of leaving Paris to return to Venice, you went away almost immediately after dinner, and I have never had the honour of seeing you since that time."

"Now I recollect you," he answered, "and I remember asking whether you were not the secretary of the embassy. But from this day we shall not forget each other again, for the mysteries which unite us are of a nature likely to establish a lasting intimacy between us."

The amiable couple were not long before they felt thoroughly at ease, and we sat down to supper, of which, of course, I did the honours. The ambassador, a fine connoisseur in wines, found mine excellent, and was delighted to hear that I had them from Count Algarotti, who was reputed as having the best cellar in Venice.

My supper was delicate and abundant, and my manners towards my handsome guests were those of a private individual receiving his sovereign and his mistress. I saw that M——M——was charmed with the respect with which I treated her, and with my conversation, which evidently interested the ambassador highly. The serious character of a first meeting did not prevent the utterance of witty jests, for in that respect M. de Bernis was a true Frenchman. I have travelled much, I have deeply studied men, individually and in a body, but I have never met with true sociability except in Frenchmen; they alone know how to jest, and it is rare, delicate, refined jesting, which animates conversation and makes society charming.

During our delightful supper wit was never wanting, and the amiable M——M——led the conversation to the romantic combination which had given her occasion to know me. Naturally, she proceeded to speak of my passion for C—— C——, and she gave such an interesting description of that young girl that the ambassador listened with as much attention as if he had never seen the object of it. But that was his part, for he was not aware that I had been informed of his having witnessed from his hiding-place my silly interview with C—— C——. He told M—— M—— that he would have been delighted if she had brought her young friend to sup with us.

"That would be running too great a risk," answered the cunning nun, "but if you approve of it," she added, looking at me, "I can make you sup with her at my casino, for we sleep in the same room."

That offer surprised me much, but it was not the moment to shew it, so I replied:

"It is impossible, madam, to add anything to the pleasure of your society, yet I confess I should be pleased if you could contrive to do us that great favour:"

"Well, I will think of it."

"But," observed the ambassador, "if I am to be one of the party, I think it would be right to apprize the young lady of it."

"It is not necessary, for I will write to her to agree to whatever madam may propose to her. I will do so to-morrow."

I begged the ambassador to prepare himself with a good stock of indulgence for a girl of fifteen who had no experience of the world. In the course of the evening I related the history of O-Morphi, which greatly amused him. He entreated me to let him see her portrait. He informed me that she was still an inmate of the 'Parc-aux-cerfs', where she continued to be the delight of Louis XV, to whom she had given a child. My guests left me after midnight, highly pleased, and I remained alone.

The next morning, faithful to the promise I had made to my beautiful nun, I wrote to C—— C—— without informing her that there would be a fourth person at the projected supper, and having given my note to Laura I repaired to Muran, where I found the following letter from M—— M——:

"I could not sleep soundly, my love, if I did not ease my conscience of an unpleasant weight. Perhaps you did not approve of the 'partie carree' with our young friend, and you may not have objected out of mere politeness. Tell me the truth, dearest, for, should you not look forward to that meeting with pleasure, I can contrive to undo it without implicating you in any way; trust me for that. If, however, you have no objection to the party, it will take place as agreed. Believe me, I love your soul more than your heart—I mean than your person. Adieu."

Her fear was very natural, but out of shamefacedness I did not like to retract. M—— M—— knew me well, and as a skilful tactician she attacked my weak side.

Here is my answer:

"I expected your letter, my best beloved, and you cannot doubt it, because, as you know me thoroughly, you must be aware that I know you as well. Yes, I know your mind, and I know what idea you must entertain of mine, because I have exposed to you all my weakness and irritability by my sophisms. I do penance for it, dearest, when I think that having raised your suspicions your tenderness for me must have been weakened. Forget my visions, I beg, and be quite certain that for the future my soul will be in unison with yours. The supper must take place, it will be a pleasure for me, but let me confess that in accepting it I have shewn myself more grateful than polite. C——C—— is a novice, and I am not sorry to give her an opportunity of seeing the world. In what school could she learn better than yours? Therefore I recommend her to you, and you will please me much by continuing to shew your care and friendship towards her, and by increasing, if possible, the sum of your goodness. I fear that you may entice her to take the veil, and if she did I would never console myself. Your friend has quite captivated me; he is a superior man, and truly charming."

Thus did I wittingly deprive myself of the power of drawing back, but I was able to realize the full force of the situation. I had no difficulty in guessing that the ambassador was in love with C——C——, and that he had confessed as much to M——M——, who, not being in a position to object to it, was compelled to shew herself compliant, and to assist him in everything that could render his passion successful. She could certainly not do anything without my consent, and she had evidently considered the affair too delicate to venture upon proposing the party point-blank to me. They had, no doubt, put their heads together, so that by bringing the conversation on that subject I should find myself compelled, for the sake of politeness and perhaps of my inward feelings, to fall into the snare. The ambassador, whose profession it was to carry on intrigues skilfully, had succeeded well, and I had taken the bait as he wished. There was nothing left for me but to put a good face on the matter, not only so as not to shew myself a very silly being, but also in order not to prove myself shamefully ungrateful towards a man who had granted me unheard-of privileges. Nevertheless, the consequence of it all was likely to be some coolness in my feelings towards both my mistresses. M——M—— had become conscious of this after she had returned to the convent, and wishing to screen herself from all responsibility she had lost no time in writing to me that she would cause the projected supper to be abandoned, in case I should disapprove of it, but she knew very well that I would not accept her offer. Self-love is a stronger passion even than jealousy; it does not allow a man who has some pretension to wit to shew himself jealous, particularly towards a person who is not tainted by that base passion, and has proved it.

The next day, having gone early to the casino, I found the ambassador already there, and he welcomed me in the most friendly manner. He told me that, if he had known me in Paris he would have introduced me at the court, where I should certainly have made my fortune. Now, when I think of that, I say to myself, "That might have been the case, but of what good would it have been to me?" Perhaps I should have fallen a victim of the Revolution, like so many others. M. de Bernis himself would have been one of those victims if Fate had not allowed him to die in Rome in 1794. He died there unhappy, although wealthy, unless his feelings had undergone a complete change before his death, and I do not believe it.

I asked him whether he liked Venice, and he answered that he could not do otherwise than like that city, in which he enjoyed excellent health, and in which, with plenty of money, life could be enjoyed better than anywhere else.

"But I do not expect," he added, "to be allowed to keep this embassy very long. Be kind enough to let that remain between us. I do not wish to make M—— M—— unhappy."

We were conversing in all confidence when M—— M—— arrived with her young friend, who showed her surprise at seeing another man with me, but I encouraged her by the most tender welcome; and she recovered all her composure when she saw the delight of the stranger at being answered by her in good French. It gave us both an opportunity of paying the warmest compliments to the mistress who had taught her so well.

C—— C—— was truly charming; her looks, bright and modest at the same time, seemed to say to me, "You must belong to me:" I wished to see her shine before our friends; and I contrived to conquer a cowardly feeling of jealousy which, in spite of myself, was beginning to get hold of me. I took care to make her talk on such subjects as I knew to be familiar to her. I developed her natural intelligence, and had the satisfaction of seeing her admired.

Applauded, flattered, animated by the satisfaction she could read in my eyes, C—— C—— appeared a prodigy to M. de Bernis, and, oh! what a contradiction of the human heart! I was pleased, yet I trembled lest he should fall in love with her! What an enigma! I was intent myself upon a work which would have caused me to murder any man who dared to undertake it.

During the supper, which was worthy of a king, the ambassador treated C—— C—— with the most delicate attentions. Wit, cheerfulness, decent manners, attended our delightful party, and did not expel the gaiety and the merry jests with which a Frenchman knows how to season every conversation.

An observing critic who, without being acquainted with us, wished to guess whether love was present at our happy party, might have suspected, perhaps, but he certainly could not have affirmed, that it was there. M—— M—— treated the ambassador as a friend. She shewed no other feeling towards me than that of deep esteem, and she behaved to C—— C—— with the tender affection of a sister. M. de Bernis was kind, polite, and amiable with M—— M——, but he never ceased to take the greatest interest in every word uttered by C—— C——, who played her part to perfection, because she had only to follow her own nature, and, that nature being beautiful, C—— C—— could not fail to be most charming.

We had passed five delightful hours, and the ambassador seemed more pleased even than any of us. M—— M—— had the air of a person satisfied with her own work, and I was playing the part of an approving spectator. C—— C—— looked highly pleased at having secured the general approbation, and there was, perhaps, a slight feeling of vanity in her arising from the special attention which the ambassador had bestowed on her. She looked at me, smiling, and I could easily understand the language of her soul, by which she wished to tell me that she felt perfectly well the difference between the society in which she was then, and that in which her brother had given us such a disgusting specimen of his depravity.

After midnight it was time to think of our departure, and M. de Bernis undertook all the complimentary part. Thanking M—— M—— for the most agreeable supper he had ever made in his life, he contrived to make her offer a repetition of it for two days afterwards, and he asked me, for the sake of appearance, whether I should not find as much delight in that second meeting as himself. Could he have any doubt of my answering affirmatively? I believe not, for I had placed myself under the necessity of being compliant. All being agreed, we parted company.

The next day, when I thought of that exemplary supper, I had no difficulty in guessing what the ultimate result would be. The ambassador owed his great fortune entirely to the fair sex, because he possessed to the highest degree the art of coddling love; and as his nature was eminently voluptuous he found his advantage in it, because he knew how to call desires into existence, and this procured him enjoyments worthy of his delicate taste. I saw that he was deeply in love with C——— C———, and I was far from supposing him the man to be satisfied with looking at her lovely eyes. He certainly had some plan arranged, and M——— M———, in spite of all her honesty, was the prime manager of it. I knew that she would carry it on with such delicate skill that I should not see any evidence of it. Although I did not feel disposed to shew more compliance than was strictly just, I foresaw that in the end I should be the dupe, and my poor C——— C——— the victim, of a cunningly-contrived trick. I could not make up my mind either to consent with a good grace, or to throw obstacles in the way, and, believing my dear little wife incapable of abandoning herself to anything likely to displease me, I allowed myself to be taken off my guard, and to rely upon the difficulty of seducing her. Stupid calculation! Self-love and shamefacedness prevented me from using my common sense. At all events, that intrigue kept me in a state of fever because I was afraid of its consequences, and yet curiosity mastered me to such an extent that I was longing for the result. I knew very well that a second edition of the supper did not imply that the same play would be performed a second time, and I foresaw that the changes would be strongly marked. But I thought myself bound in honour not to retract. I could not lead the intrigue, but I believed myself sufficiently skilful to baffle all their manoeuvrings.

After all those considerations, however, considerations which enabled me to assume the countenance of false bravery, the inexperience of C——— C———, who, in spite of all the knowledge she had lately acquired, was only a novice, caused me great anxiety. It was easy to abuse her natural wish to be polite, but that fear gave way very soon before the confidence I had in M——— M———s delicacy. I thought that, having seen how I had spent six hours with that young girl, knowing for a certainty that I intended to marry her, M——— M———would never be guilty of such base treason. All these thoughts, worthy only of a weak and bashful jealousy, brought no conclusive decision. I had to follow the current and watch events.

At the appointed time I repaired to the casino, where I found my two lovely friends sitting by the fire.

"Good evening, my two divinities, where is our charming Frenchman?"

"He has not arrived yet," answered M——— M———, "but he will doubtless soon be here."

I took off my mask, and sitting between them, I gave them a thousand kisses, taking good care not to shew any preference, and although I knew that they were aware of the unquestionable right I had upon both of them, I kept within the limits of the utmost decency. I congratulated them upon the mutual inclination they felt for each other, and I saw that they were pleased not to have to blush on that account.

More than one hour was spent in gallant and friendly conversation, without my giving any satisfaction to my burning desires. M—— M—— attracted me more than C—— C——, but I would not for the world have offended the charming girl. M—— M—— was beginning to shew some anxiety about the absence of M. de Bernis, when the door-keeper brought her a note from him.

"A courier," he wrote, "who arrived two hours ago, prevents my being happy to-night, for I am compelled to pass it in answering the dispatches I have received. I trust that you will forgive and pity me. May I hope that you will kindly grant me on Friday the pleasure of which I am so unfortunately deprived to-day? Let me know your answer by to-morrow. I wish ardently, in that case, to find you with the same guests, to whom I beg you will present my affectionate compliments."

"Well," said M—— M——, "it is not his fault. We will sup without him. Will you come on Friday?"

"Yes, with the greatest pleasure. But what is the matter with you, dear C—— C——? You look sad."

"Sad, no, unless it should be for the sake of my friend, for I have never seen a more polite and more obliging gentleman."

"Very well, dear, I am glad he has rendered you so sensible."

"What do you mean? Could anyone be insensible to his merit?"

"Better still, but I agree with you. Only tell me if you love him?"

"Well, even if I loved him, do you think I would go and tell him? Besides, I am certain that he loves my friend."

So saying, she sat down on M—— M——'s knee, calling her her own little wife, and my two beauties began to bestow on one another caresses which made me laugh heartily. Far from troubling their sport, I excited them, in order to enjoy a spectacle with which I had long been acquainted.

M—— M—— took up a book full of the most lascivious engravings, and said, with a significant glance in my direction:

"Do you wish me to have a fire lighted in the alcove?"

I understood her, and replied:

"You would oblige me, for the bed being large we can all three sleep comfortably in it."

I guessed that she feared my suspecting the ambassador of enjoying from the mysterious closet the sight of our amorous trio, and she wished to destroy that suspicion by her proposal.

The table having been laid in front of the alcove, supper was served, and we all did honour to it. We were all blessed with a devouring appetite. While M—— M—— was teaching her friend how to mix punch, I was admiring with delight the progress made in beauty by C—— C——.

"Your bosom," I said to her, "must have become perfect during the last nine months."

"It is like mine," answered M—— M——, "would you like to see for yourself?"

Of course I did not refuse. M—— M—— unlaced her friend, who made no resistance, and performing afterwards the same office upon herself, in less than two minutes I was admiring four rivals contending for the golden apple like the three goddesses, and which would have set at defiance the handsome Paris himself to adjudge the prize without injustice. Need I say what an ardent fire that ravishing sight sent coursing through my veins? I placed immediately an the table the Academie des Dames, and pointed out a certain position to M—— M——, who, understanding my wishes, said to C—— C—— :

"Will you, darling, represent that group with me?"

A look of compliance was C—— C——'s only answer; she was not yet inured to amorous pleasures as much as her lovely teacher. While I was laughing with delight, the two friends were getting ready, and in a few minutes we were all three in bed, and in a state of nature. At first, satisfied with enjoying the sight of the barren contest of my two bacchanalians, I was amused by their efforts and by the contrast of colours, for one was dark and the other fair, but soon, excited myself, and consumed by all the fire of voluptuousness, I threw myself upon them, and I made them, one after the other, almost faint away from the excess of love and enjoyment.

Worn out and satiated with pleasure, I invited them to take some rest. We slept until we were awakened by the alarum, which I had taken care to set at four o'clock. We were certain of turning to good account the two hours we had then to spare before parting company, which we did at the dawn of day, humiliated at having to confess our exhaustion, but highly pleased with each other, and longing for a renewal of our delightful pleasures.

The next day, however, when I came to think of that rather too lively night, during which, as is generally the case, Love had routed Reason, I felt some remorse. M—— M—— wanted to convince me of her love, and for that purpose she had combined all the virtues which I attached to my own affection—namely, honour, delicacy, and truth, but her temperament, of which her mind was the slave, carried her towards excess, and she prepared everything in order to give way to it, while she awaited the opportunity of making me her accomplice. She was coaxing love to make it compliant, and to succeed in mastering it, because her heart, enslaved by her senses, never reproached her. She likewise tried to deceive herself by endeavouring to forget that I might complain of having been surprised. She knew that to utter such a complaint I would have to acknowledge myself weaker or less courageous than she was, and she relied upon my being ashamed to make such a confession. I had no doubt whatever that the absence of the ambassador had been arranged and concerted beforehand. I could see still further, for it seemed evident to me that the two conspirators had foreseen that I would guess the artifice, and that, feeling stung to the quick, in spite of all my regrets, I would not shew myself less generous than they had been themselves. The ambassador having first procured me a delightful night, how could I refuse to let him enjoy as pleasant a one? My friends had argued very well, for, in spite of all the objections of my mind, I saw that I could not on my side put any obstacle in their way. C—— C—— was no impediment to them. They were certain of conquering her the moment she was not hindered by my presence. It rested entirely with M—— M——, who had perfect control over her. Poor girl! I saw her on the high road to debauchery, and it was my own doing! I sighed when I thought how little I had spared them in our last orgie, and what would become of me if both of them should happen to be, by my doing, in such a position as to be compelled to run away from the convent? I could imagine both of them thrown upon my hands, and the prospect was not particularly agreeable. It would be an 'embarras de richesse'. In this miserable contest between reason and prejudice, between nature and sentiment, I could not make up my mind either to go to the supper or to remain absent from it. "If I go," said I to myself, "that night will pass with perfect decency, but I shall prove myself very ridiculous, jealous, ungrateful, and even wanting in common politeness:

if I remain absent, C——— C——— is lost, at least, in my estimation, for I feel that my love will no longer exist, and then good-bye to all idea of a marriage with her." In the perplexity of mind in which I found myself, I felt a want of something more certain than mere probabilities to base my decision upon. I put on my mask, and repaired to the mansion of the French ambassador. I addressed myself to the gate-keeper, saying that I had a letter for Versailles, and that I would thank him to deliver it to the courier when he went back to France with his excellency's dispatches.

"But, sir," answered the man, "we have not had a special courier for the last two months."

"What? Did not a special cabinet messenger arrive here last night?"

"Then he must have come in through the garret window or down the chimney, for, on the word of an honest man, none entered through the gate."

"But the ambassador worked all night?"

"That may be, sir, but not here, for his excellency dined with the Spanish ambassador, and did not return till very late."

I had guessed rightly. I could no longer entertain any doubt. It was all over; I could not draw back without shame. C——— C——— must resist, if the game was distasteful to her; no violence would of course be offered to her. The die was cast!

Towards evening I went to the casino of Muran, and wrote a short note to M——— M———, requesting her to excuse me if some important business of M. de Bragadin's prevented me from spending the night with her and with our two friends, to whom I sent my compliments as well as my apologies. After that I returned to Venice, but in rather an unpleasant mood; to divert myself I went to the gaming table, and lost all night.

Two days afterwards, being certain that a letter from M——— M——— awaited me at Muran, I went over, and the door-keeper handed me a parcel in which I found a note from my nun and a letter from C——— C———, for everything was now in common between them.

Here is C——— C———'s letter."

"We were very sorry, dearest friend, when we heard that we should not have the happiness of seeing you. My dear M——— M———'s friend came shortly afterwards, and when he read your note he likewise expressed his deep regret. We expected to have a very dull supper, but the witty sayings of that gentleman enlivened us and you cannot imagine of what follies we were guilty after partaking of some champagne punch. Our friend had become as gay as ourselves, and we spent the night in trios, not very fatiguing, but very pleasant. I can assure you that that man deserves to be loved, but he must acknowledge himself inferior to you in everything. Believe me, dearest, I shall ever love you, and you must for ever remain the master of my heart."

In spite of all my vexation, that letter made me laugh, but the note of M—— M—— was much more singular. Here are the contents of it:

"I am certain, my own beloved, that you told a story out of pure politeness, but you had guessed that I expected you to do so. You have made our friend a splendid present in exchange for the one he made you when he did not object to his M—— M—— bestowing her heart upon you. You possess that heart entirely, dearest, and you would possess it under all circumstances, but how sweet it is to flavour the pleasures of love with the charms of friendship! I was sorry not to see you, but I knew that if you had come we would not have had much enjoyment; for our friend, notwithstanding all his wit, is not exempt from some natural prejudices. As for C—— C——, her mind is now quite as free of them as our own, and I am glad she owes it to me. You must feel thankful to me for having completed her education, and for rendering her in every way worthy of you. I wish you had been hiding in the closet, where I am certain you would have spent some delightful hours. On Wednesday next I shall be yours, and all alone with you in your casino in Venice; let me know whether you will be at the usual hour near the statue of the hero Colleoni. In case you should be prevented, name any other day."

I had to answer those two letters in the same spirit in which they had been written, and in spite of all the bitter feelings which were then raging in my heart, my answers were to be as sweet as honey. I was in need of great courage, but I said to myself: "George Dandin, tu las voulu!" I could not refuse to pay the penalty of my own deeds, and I have never been able to ascertain whether the shame I felt was what is called shamefacedness. It is a problem which I leave to others.

In my letter to C—— C—— I had the courage, or the effrontery, to congratulate her, and to encourage her to imitate M—— M——, the best model, I said, I could propose to her.

I wrote to my nun that I would be punctual at the appointment near the statue, and amidst many false compliments, which ought to have betrayed the true state of my heart, I told her that I admired the perfect education she had given to C—— C——, but that I congratulated myself upon having escaped the torture I should have suffered in the mysterious observatory, for I felt that I could not have borne it.

On the Wednesday I was punctual at the rendezvous, and I had not to wait long for M—— M——, who came disguised in male attire. "No theatre to-night," she said to me; "let us go to the 'ridotto', to lose or double our money." She had six hundred sequins. I had about one hundred. Fortune turned her back upon us, and we lost all. I expected that we would then leave that cutthroat place, but M—— M——, having left me for a minute, came back with three hundred sequins which had been given to her by her friend, whom she knew where to find. That money given by love or by friendship brought her luck for a short time, and she soon won back all we had lost, but in our greediness or imprudence we continued to play, and finally we lost our last sequin.

When we could play no longer, M—— M—— said to me,

"Now that we need not fear thieves, let us go to our supper."

That woman, religious and a Free-thinker, a libertine and gambler, was wonderful in all she did. She had just lost five hundred pounds, and she was as completely at her ease as if she had won a very large sum. It is true that the money she had just lost had not cost her much.

As soon as we were alone, she found me sad and low-spirited, although I tried hard not to appear so, but, as for her, always the same, she was handsome, brilliant, cheerful, and amorous.

She thought she would bring back my spirits by giving me the fullest particulars of the night she had passed with C—— C—— and her friend, but she ought to have guessed that she was going the wrong way. That is a very common error, it comes from the mind, because people imagine that what they feel themselves others must feel likewise.

I was on thorns, and I tried everything to avoid that subject, and to lead the conversation into a different channel, for the amorous particulars, on which she was dwelling with apparent delight, vexed me greatly, and spite causing coldness, I was afraid of not playing my part very warmly in the amorous contest which was at hand. When a lover doubts his own strength, he may almost always be sure that he will fail in his efforts.

After supper we went to bed in the alcove, where the beauty, the mental and physical charms, the grace and the ardour of my lovely nun, cast all my bad temper to the winds, and soon restored me to my usual good-spirits. The nights being shorter we spent two hours in the most delightful pleasures, and then parted, satisfied and full of love.

Before leaving, M—— M—— asked me to go to her casino, to take some money and to play, taking her for my partner. I did so. I took all the gold I found, and playing the martingale, and doubling my stakes continuously, I won every day during the remainder of the carnival. I was fortunate enough never to lose the sixth card, and, if I had lost it, I should have been without money to play, for I had two thousand sequins on that card. I congratulated myself upon having increased the treasure of my dear mistress, who wrote to me that, for the sake of civility, we ought to have a supper 'en partie carree' on Shrove Monday. I consented.

That supper was the last I ever had in my life with C—— C——. She was in excellent spirits, but I had made up my mind, and as I paid all my attentions to M—— M——, C—— C—— imitated my example without difficulty, and she devoted herself wholly to her new lover.

Foreseeing that we would, a little later, be all of us in each other's way, I begged M—— M—— to arrange everything so that we could be apart, and she contrived it marvellously well.

After supper, the ambassador proposed a game of faro, which our beauties did not know; he called for cards, and placed one hundred Louis on the table before him; he dealt, and took care to make C—— C—— win the whole of that sum. It was the best way to make her accept it as pin-money. The young girl, dazzled by so much gold, and not knowing what to do with it, asked her friend to take care of it for her until such time as she should leave the convent to get married.

When the game was over, M—— M—— complained of a headache, and said that she would go to bed in the alcove: she asked me to come and lull her to sleep. We thus left the new lovers free to be as gay as they chose. Six hours afterwards, when the alarum warned us that it was time to part, we found them asleep in each other's embrace. I had myself passed an amorous and quiet night, pleased with M—— M——, and with out giving one thought to C—— C——.

II

M. De Bernis Goes Away Leaving Me the Use of His
Casino—His Good Advice: How I Follow It—Peril of
M. M. and Myself—Mr. Murray, the English Ambassador—
Sale of the Casino and End of Our Meetings—Serious
Illness of M. M.—Zorzi and Condulmer—Tonnie

Though the infidelities of C—— C—— made me look at her with
other eyes than before, and I had now no intention of making her
the companion of my life, I could not help feeling that it had rested with
me to stop her on the brink of the stream, and I therefore considered it
my duty always to be her friend.

If I had been more logical, the resolution I took with respect to her
would doubtless have been of another kind. I should have said to myself:
After seducing her, I myself have set the example of infidelity; I have
bidden her to follow blindly the advice of her friend, although I knew
that the advice and the example of M——M——would end in her ruin;
I had insulted, in the most grievous manner, the delicacy of my mistress,
and that before her very eyes, and after all this how could I ask a weak
woman to do what a man, priding himself on his strength, would shrink
from at tempting? I should have stood self-condemned, and have felt
that it was my duty to remain the same to her, but flattering myself that
I was overcoming mere prejudices, I was in fact that most degraded of
slaves, he who uses his strength to crush the weak.

The day after Shrove Tuesday, going to the casino of Muran, I found
there a letter from M——M——, who gave me two pieces of bad news:
that C—— C—— had lost her mother, and that the poor girl was in
despair; and that the lay-sister, whose rheum was cured, had returned
to take her place. Thus C—— C—— was deprived of her friend at a
time when she would have given her consolation, of which she stood in
great need. C——C——, it seemed, had gone to share the rooms of her
aunt, who, being very fond of her, had obtained permission from the
superior. This circumstance would prevent the ambassador taking any
more suppers with her, and I should have been delighted if chance had
put this obstacle in his path a few days sooner.

All these misfortunes seemed of small account com pared with what
I was afraid of, for C—— C—— might have to pay the price for her

pleasures, and I so far regarded myself as the origin of her unhappiness as to feel bound never to abandon her, and this might have involved me in terrible complications.

M—— M—— asked me to sup with her and her lover on the following Monday. I went and found them both sad—he for the loss of his new mistress, and she because she had no longer a friend to make the seclusion of the convent pleasant.

About midnight M. de Bemis left us, saying in a melancholy manner that he feared he should be obliged to pass several months in Vienna on important diplomatic business. Before parting we agreed to sup together every Friday.

When we were alone M—— M—— told me that the ambassador would be obliged to me if in the future I would come to the casino two hours later. I understood that the good-natured and witty profligate had a very natural prejudice against indulging his amorous feelings except when he was certain of being alone.

M. de Bemis came to all our suppers till he left for Vienna, and always went away at midnight. He no longer made use of his hiding-place, partly because we now only lay in the recess, and partly because, having had time to make love before my arrival, his desires were appeased. M—— M—— always found me amorous. My love, indeed, was even hotter than it had been, since, only seeing her once a week and remaining faithful to her, I had always an abundant harvest to gather in. C—— C——'s letters which she brought to me softened me to tears, for she said that after the loss of her mother she could not count upon the friendship of any of her relations. She called me her sole friend, her only protector, and in speaking of her grief in not being able to see me any more whilst she remained in the convent, she begged me to remain faithful to her dear friend.

On Good Friday, when I got to the casino, I found the lovers over-whelmed with grief. Supper was served, but the ambassador, downcast and absent, neither ate nor spoke; and M—— M—— was like a statue that moves at intervals by some mechanism. Good sense and ordinary politeness prevented me from asking any questions, but on M—— M—— leaving us together, M. de Bemis told me that she was distressed, and with reason, since he was obliged to set out for Vienna fifteen days after Easter. "I may tell you confidentially," he added, "that I believe I shall scarcely be able to return, but she must not be told, as she would be in despair." M—— M—— came back in a few minutes, but it was easy to see that she had been weeping.

After some commonplace conversation, M. de Bernis, seeing M——
M—— still low-spirited, said,

"Do not grieve thus, sweetheart, go I must, but my return is a matter
of equal certainty when I have finished the important business which
summons me to Vienna. You will still have the casino, but, dearest,
both friendship and prudence make me advise you not to come here in
my absence, for after I have left Venice I cannot depend upon the faith
of the gondoliers in my service, and I suspect our friend here cannot
flatter himself on his ability to get reliable ones. I may also tell you that
I have strong reasons for suspecting that our intercourse is known to the
State Inquisitors, who conceal their knowledge for political reasons, but
I fancy the secret would soon come to light when I am no longer here,
and when the nun who connives at your departure from the convent
knows that it is no longer for me that you leave it. The only people
whom I would trust are the housekeeper and his wife. I shall order
them, before I go, to look upon our friend here as myself, and you can
make your arrangements with them. I trust all will go well till my return,
if you will only behave discreetly. I will write to you under cover of the
housekeeper, his wife will give you my letters as before, and in the same
way you may reply. I must needs go, dearest one, but my heart is with
you, and I leave you, till my return, in the hands of a friend, whom I
rejoice to have known. He loves you, he has a heart and knowledge of
the world, and he will not let you make any mistakes."

M—— M—— was so affected by what the ambassador had said that
she entreated us to let her go, as she wished to be alone and to lie down.
As she went we agreed to sup together on the following Thursday.

As soon as we were alone the ambassador impressed me with the
absolute necessity of concealing from her that he was going to return
no more. "I am going," said he, "to work in concert with the Austrian
cabinet on a treaty which will be the talk of Europe. I entreat you to
write to me unreservedly, and as a friend, and if you love our common
mistress, have a care for her honour, and above all have the strength of
mind to resist all projects which are certain to involve you in misfortune,
and which will be equally fatal to both. You know what happened to
Madame de Riva, a nun in the convent of St.——. She had to disappear
after it became known that she was with child, and M. de Frulai, my
predecessor, went mad, and died shortly after. J. J. Rousseau told me
that he died of poison, but he is a visionary who sees the black side of
everything. For my part, I believe that he died of grief at not being able

to do anything for the unfortunate woman, who afterwards procured a dispensation from her vows from the Pope, and having got married is now living at Padua without any position in society.

"Let the prudent and loyal friend master the lover: go and see M—— M—— sometimes in the parlour of the convent, but not here, or the boatmen will betray you. The knowledge which we both have that the girls are in a satisfactory condition is a great alleviation to my distress, but you must confess that you have been very imprudent. You have risked a terrible misfortune; consider the position you would have been in, for I am sure you would not have abandoned her. She had an idea that the danger might be overcome by means of drugs but I convinced her that she was mistaken. In God's name, be discreet in the future, and write to me fully, for I shall always be interested in her fate, both from duty and sentiment."

We returned together to Venice, where we separated, and I passed the rest of the night in great distress. In the morning I wrote to the fair afflicted, and whilst endeavouring to console her to the best of my ability, I tried to impress on her the necessity for prudence and the avoidance of such escapades as might eventually ruin us.

Next day I received her reply, every word of which spelt despair. Nature had given her a disposition which had become so intensified by indulgence that the cloister was unbearable to her, and I foresaw the hard fights I should have to undergo.

We saw each other the Thursday after Easter, and I told her that I should not come to the casino before midnight. She had had four hours to pass with her lover in tears and regrets, amongst which she had often cursed her cruel fate and the foolish resolution which made her take the veil. We supped together, and although the meal was a rich and delicate one we did it little honour. When we had finished, the ambassador left, entreating me to remain, which I did, without thinking at all of the pleasures of a party of two, for Love lighteth not his torch at the hearts of two lovers who are full of grief and sorrow. M—— M—— had grown thin, and her condition excited my pity and shut out all other feelings. I held her a long time in my arms, covering her with tender and affectionate kisses, but I shewed no intention of consoling her by amusements in which her spirit could not have taken part. She said, before we parted, that I had shewn myself a true lover, and she asked me to consider myself from henceforth as her only friend and protector.

Next week, when we were together as usual, M. de Bemis called the housekeeper just before supper, and in his presence executed a deed in my behalf, which he made him sign. In this document he transferred to me all rights over the contents of the casino, and charged him to consider me in all things as his master.

We arranged to sup together two days after, to make our farewells, but on my arrival I found by herself, standing up, and pale as death, or rather as white as a statue of Carrara marble.

"He is gone," she said, "and he leaves me to your care. Fatal being, whom perchance I shall see no more, whom I thought I loved but as a friend, now you are lost to me I see my mistake. Before I knew him I was not happy, but neither was I unhappy as I now am."

I passed the whole night beside her, striving by the most delicate attentions to soften her grief, but with out success. Her character, as abandoned to sorrow as to pleasure, was displayed to me during that long and weary night. She told me at what hour I should come to the convent parlour, the next day, and on my arrival I was delighted to find her not quite so sad. She shewed me a letter which her lover had written to her from Trevisa, and she then told me that I must come and see her twice a week, warning me that she would be accompanied sometimes by one nun and sometimes by another, for she foresaw that my visits would become the talk of the convent, when it became known that I was the individual who used to go to mass at their church. She therefore told me to give in another name, to prevent C—— C——'s aunt from becoming suspicious.

"Nevertheless," she added, "this will not prevent my coming alone when I have any matter of importance to communicate to you. Promise me, sweetheart, to sup and sleep at the casino at least once a week, and write me a note each time by the housekeeper's wife."

I made no difficulty in promising her that much.

We thus passed a fortnight quietly enough, as she was happy again, and her amorous inclinations had returned in full force. About this time she gave me a piece of news which delighted me—namely, that C—— C—— had no longer anything to fear.

Full of amorous wishes and having to be content with the teasing pleasure of seeing one another through a wretched grating, we racked our brains to find out some way to be alone together to do what we liked, without any risk.

"I am assured," she said, "of the good faith of the gardener's sister. I can go out and come in without fear of being seen, for the little door leading to the convent is not overlooked by any window—indeed it is thought to be walled up. Nobody can see me crossing the garden to the little stream, which is considered unnavigable. All we want is a one-oared gondola, and I cannot believe that with the help of money you will be unable to find a boatman on whom we may rely."

I understood from these expressions that she suspected me of becoming cold towards her, and this suspicion pierced me to the heart.

"Listen," said I, "I will be the boatman myself. I will come to the quay, pass by the little door, and you shall lead me to your room where I will pass the whole night with you, and the day, too, if you think you can hide me."

"That plan," said she, "makes me shudder. I tremble at the danger to which you might be exposed. No, I should be too unfortunate if I were to be the cause of your misfortune, but, as you can row, come in the boat, let me know the time as closely as possible; the trusty woman will be on the watch, and I will not keep you four minutes waiting. I will get into the boat, we will go to our beloved casino, and then we shall be happy without fearing anything."

"I will think it over."

The way I took to satisfy her was as follows: I bought a small boat, and without telling her I went one night all by myself round the island to inspect the walls of the convent on the side of the lagune. With some difficulty I made out a little door, which I judged to be the only one by which she could pass, but to go from there to the casino was no small matter, since one was obliged to fetch a wide course, and with one oar I could not do the passage in less than a quarter of an hour, and that with much toil. Nevertheless, feeling sure of success, I told my pretty nun of the plan, and never was news received with so much pleasure. We set our watches together, and fixed our meeting for the Friday following.

On the day appointed, an hour before sunset, I betook myself to St. Francis de la Vigne, where I kept my boat, and having set it in order and dressed myself as a boatman, I got upon the poop and held a straight course for the little door, which opened the moment I arrived. M——M—— came out wrapped in a cloak, and someone shutting the door after her she got on board my frail bark, and in a quarter of an hour we were at the casino. M——M—— made haste to go in, but I stayed to belay my boat with a lock and chain against thieves, who pass the night pleasantly by stealing whatever they can lay hands on.

Though I had rowed easily enough, I was in a bath of perspiration, which, however, by no means hindered my charming mistress from falling on my neck; the pleasure of meeting seemed to challenge her love, and, proud of what I had done, I enjoyed her transports.

Not dreaming that I should have any occasion for a change of linen, I had brought none with me, but she soon found a cure for this defect; for after having undressed me she dried me lovingly, gave me one of her smocks, and I found myself dressed to admiration.

We had been too long deprived of our amorous pleasures to think of taking supper before we had offered a plenteous sacrifice to love. We spent two hours in the sweetest of intoxications, our bliss seeming more acute than at our first meeting. In spite of the fire which consumed me, in spite of the ardour of my mistress, I was sufficiently master of myself to disappoint her at the critical moment, for the picture which our friend had drawn was always before my eyes. M—— M——, joyous and wanton, having me for the first time in the character of boatman, augmented our delights by her amorous caprices, but it was useless for her to try to add fuel to my flame, since I loved her better than myself.

The night was short, for she was obliged to return at three in the morning, and it struck one as we sat down to table. As the climax of ill luck a storm came on whilst we were at supper. Our hair stood on end; our only hope was founded in the nature of these squalls, which seldom last more than an hour. We were in hopes, also, that it would not leave behind it too strong a wind, as is sometimes the case, for though I was strong and sturdy I was far from having the skill or experience of a professional boatman.

In less than half an hour the storm became violent, one flash of lightning followed another, the thunder roared, and the wind grew to a gale. Yet after a heavy rain, in less than an hour, the sky cleared, but there was no moon, it being the day after the Ascension. Two o'clock stuck. I put my head out at the window, but perceive that a contrary gale is blowing.

'Ma tiranno del mar Libecchio resta.'

This Libecchio which Ariosto calls—and with good reason—the tyrant of the sea, is the southwesterly wind, which is commonly called 'Garbin' at Venice. I said nothing, but I was frightened. I told my sweetheart that we must needs sacrifice an hour of pleasure, since prudence would have it so.

"Let us set out forthwith, for if the gale gets stronger I shall not be able to double the island."

She saw my advice was not to be questioned, and taking the key of her strong box, whence she desired to get some money, she was delighted to find her store increased fourfold. She thanked me for having told her nothing about it, assuring me she would have of me nothing but my heart, and following me she got into my boat and lay down at full length so as not to hinder its motion, I got upon the poop, as full of fear as courage, and in five minutes I had the good luck to double the point. But there it was that the tyrant was waiting for me, and it was not long before I felt that my strength would not outlast that of the winds. I rowed with all my strength, but all I could do was to prevent my boat from going back. For half an hour I was in this pitiful state, and I felt my strength failing without daring to say a word. I was out of breath, but could not rest a moment, since the least relaxation would have let the boat slip a far way back, and this would have been a distance hard to recover. M——M—— lay still and silent, for she perceived I had no breath wherewith to answer her. I began to give ourselves up as lost.

At that instant I saw in the distance a barque coming swiftly towards us. What a piece of luck! I waited till she caught us up, for if I had not done so I should not have been able to make myself heard, but as soon as I saw her at my left hand, twelve feet off, I shouted, "Help! I will give two sequins!"

They lowered sail and came towards me, and on their hailing me I asked for a man to take us to the opposite point of the island. They asked a sequin in advance, I gave it them, and promised the other to the man who would get on my poop and help me to make the point. In less than ten minutes we were opposite to the little stream leading to the convent, but the secret of it was too dear to be hazarded, so as soon as we reached the point I paid my preserver and sent him back. Henceforth the wind was in our favour, and we soon got to the little door, where M——M—— landed, saying to me, "Go and sleep in the casino." I thought her advice wise, and I followed it, and having the wind behind me I got to the casino without trouble, and slept till broad day. As soon as I had risen I wrote to my dear mistress that I was well, and that we should see each other at the grating. Having taken my boat back to St. Francis, I put on my mask and went to Liston.

In the morning M——M—— came to the grating by herself, and we made all such observations as our adventures of the night would be likely to suggest, but in place of deciding to follow the advice which prudence should have given us-namely, not to expose ourselves to danger for the future, we thought ourselves extremely prudent in resolving that if we were again threatened by a storm we would set out as soon as we saw it rising. All the same we had to confess that if chance had not thrown the barque in our way we should have been obliged to return to the casino, for M—— M—— could not have got to the convent, and how could she ever have entered its walls again? I should have been forced to leave Venice with her, and that for ever. My life would have been finally and irretrievably linked with hers, and, without doubt, the various adventures which at the age of seventy-two years impel me to write these Memoirs, would never have taken place.

For the next three months we continued to meet each other once a week, always amorous, and never disturbed by the slightest accidents.

M—— M—— could not resist giving the ambassador a full account of our adventures, and I had promised to write to him, and always to write the whole truth. He replied by congratulating us on our good fortune, but he prophesied inevitable disaster if we had not the prudence to stop our intercourse.

Mr. Murray, the English ambassador, a witty and handsome man, and a great amateur of the fair sex, wine, and good cheer, then kept the fair Ancilla, who introduced me to him. This fine fellow became my friend in much the same way as M. de Bernis, the only difference being that the Frenchman liked to look on while the Englishman preferred to give the show. I was never unwelcome at their amorous battles, and the voluptuous Ancilla was delighted to have me for a witness. I never gave them the pleasure of mingling in the strife. I loved M—— M——, but I should avow that my fidelity to her was not entirely dependent on my love. Though Ancilla was handsome she inspired me with repugnance, for she was always hoarse, and complained of a sharp pain in the throat, and though her lover kept well, I was afraid of her, and not without cause, for the disease which ended the days of Francis I. of France brought her to the grave in the following autumn. A quarter of an hour before she died, her brave Briton, yielding to the lascivious requests of this new Messalina, offered in my presence the last sacrifice, in spite of a large sore on her face which made her look hideous.

This truly heroic action was known all over the town, and it was Murray himself who made it known, citing me as his witness.

This famous courtezan, whose beauty was justly celebrated, feeling herself eaten away by an internal disease, promised to give a hundred louis to a doctor named Lucchesi, who by dint of mercury undertook to cure her, but Ancilla specified on the agreement that she was not to pay the aforesaid sum till Lucchesi had offered with her an amorous sacrifice.

The doctor having done his business as well as he could wished to be paid without submitting to the conditions of the treaty, but Ancilla held her ground, and the matter was brought before a magistrate.

In England, where all agreements are binding, Ancilla would have won her case, but at Venice she lost it.

The judge, in giving sentence, said a condition, criminal per se, not fulfilled, did not invalidate an agreement—a sentence abounding in wisdom, especially in this instance.

Two months before this woman had become disgusting, my friend M. Memmo, afterwards procurator, asked me to take him to her house. In the height of the conversation, what should come but a gondola, and we saw Count Rosemberg, the ambassador from Vienna, getting out of it. M. Memmo was thunderstruck (for a Venetian noble conversing with a foreign ambassador becomes guilty of treason to the state), and ran in hot haste from Ancilla's room, I after him, but on the stair he met the ambassador, who, seeing his distress, burst into a laugh, and passed on. I got directly into M. Memmo's gondola, and we went forthwith to M. Cavalli, secretary to the State Inquisitors. M. Memmo could have taken no better course to avoid the troublesome consequences which this fatal meeting might have had, and he was very glad that I was with him to testify to his innocence and to the harmlessness of the occurrence.

M. Cavalli received M. Memmo with a smile, and told him he did well to come to confession without wasting any time. M. Memmo, much astonished at this reception, told him the brief history of the meeting, and the secretary replied with a grave air that he had no doubt as to the truth of his story, as the circumstances were in perfect correspondence with what he knew of the matter.

We came away extremely puzzled at the secretary's reply, and discussed the subject for some time, but then we came to the conclusion that M. Cavalli could have had no positive knowledge of the matter before we came, and that he only spoke as he did from the instinct of an Inquisitor, who likes it to be understood that nothing is hid from him for a moment.

After the death of Ancilla, Mr. Murray remained without a titular mistress, but, fluttering about like a butterfly, he had, one after another, the prettiest girls in Venice. This good-natured Epicurean set out for Constantinople two years later, and was for twenty years the ambassador of the Court of St. James at the Sublime Porte. He returned to Venice in 1778 with the intention of ending his days there, far from affairs of state, but he died in the lazaretto eight days before the completion of his quarantine.

At play fortune continued to favour me; my commerce with M——M—— could not be discovered now that I was my own waterman; and the nuns who were in the secret were too deeply involved not to keep it. I led them a merry life, but I foresaw that as soon as M. de Bernis decided to let M——M—— know that he would not return to Venice, he would recall his people, and we should then have the casino no longer. I knew, besides, that when the rough season came on it would be impossible for me by myself to continue our voyages.

The first Monday in October, when the theatres are opened and masks may be worn, I went to St. Francis to get my boat, and thence to Muran for my mistress, afterwards making for the casino. The nights were now long enough for us to have ample time for enjoyment, so we began by making an excellent supper, and then devoted ourselves to the worship of Love and Sleep. Suddenly, in the midst of a moment of ecstasy, I heard a noise in the direction of the canal, which aroused my suspicions, and I rushed to the window. What was my astonishment and anger to see a large boat taking mine in tow! Nevertheless, without giving way to my passion, I shouted to the robbers that I would give them ten sequins if they would be kind enough to return me my boat.

A shout of laughter was all the reply they made, and not believing what I said they continued their course. What was I to do? I dared not cry, "Stop thief!" and not being endued with the power of walking on the water dry-footed, I could not give chase to the robbers. I was in the utmost distress, and for the moment M——M—— shewed signs of terror, for she did not see how I could remedy this disaster.

I dressed myself hastily, giving no more thoughts to love, my only comfort being that I had still two hours to get the indispensable boat, should it cost me a hundred sequins. I should have been in no perplexity if I had been able to take one, but the gondoliers would infallibly make proclamation over the whole of Muran that they had taken a nun to such a convent, and all would have been lost.

The only way, then, that was open to me was either to buy a boat or to steal one. I put my pistols and dagger in my pocket, took some money, and with an oar on my shoulder set out.

The robbers had filed the chain of my boat with a silent file; this I could not do, and I could only reckon on having the good luck to find a boat moored with cords.

Coming to the large bridge I saw boats and to spare, but there were people on the quay, and I would not risk taking one. Seeing a tavern open at the end of the quay I ran like a madman, and asked if there were any boatmen there; the drawer told me there were two, but that they were drunk. I came up to them, and said, "Who will take me to Venice for eighty sous?"

"I," and "I," and they began to quarrel as to who should go. I quieted them by giving forty sous to the more drunken of the two, and I went out with the other.

As soon as we were on our way, I said,

"You are too drunk to take me, lend me your boat, and I will give it you back to-morrow."

"I don't know you."

"I will deposit ten sequins, but your boat is not worth that. Who will be your surety?"

He took me back to the tavern, and the drawer went bail for him. Well pleased, I took my man to the boat, and having furnished it with a second oar and two poles he went away, chuckling at having made a good bargain, while I was as glad to have had the worst of it. I had been an hour away, and on entering the casino found my dear M—— M—— in an agony, but as soon as she saw my beaming face all the laughter came back on hers. I took her to the convent, and then went to St. Francis, where the keeper of the boathouse looked as if he thought me a fool, when I told him that I had trucked away my boat for the one I had with me. I put on my mask, and went forthwith to my lodging and to bed, for these annoyances had been too much for me.

About this time my destiny made me acquainted with a nobleman called Mark Antony Zorzi, a man of parts and famous for his skill in writing verses in the Venetian dialect. Zorzi, who was very fond of the play, and desired to offer a sacrifice to Thalia, wrote a comedy which the audience took the liberty of hissing; but having persuaded himself that his piece only failed through the conspiracies of the Abbe Chiari, who wrote for the Theatre of St. Angelo, he declared open war against all the abbe's plays.

I felt no reluctance whatever to visit M. Zorzi, for he possessed an excellent cook and a charming wife. He knew that I did not care for Chiari as an author, and M. Zorzi had in his pay people who, without pity, rhyme, or reason, hissed all the compositions of the ecclesiastical playwright. My part was to criticise them in hammer verses—a kind of doggerel then much in fashion, and Zorzi took care to distribute my lucubrations far and wide. These manoeuvres made me a powerful enemy in the person of M. Condulmer, who liked me none the better for having all the appearance of being in high favour with Madame Zorzi, to whom before my appearance he had paid diligent court. This M. Condulmer was to be excused for not caring for me, for, having a large share in the St. Angelo Theatre, the failure of the abbe's pieces was a loss to him, as the boxes had to be let at a very low rent, and all men are governed by interested motives.

This M. Condulmer was sixty years old, but with all the greenness of youth he was still fond of women, gaming, and money, and he was, in fact, a money-lender, but he knew how to pass for a saint, as he took care to go to mass every morning at St. Mark's, and never omitted to shed tears before the crucifix. The following year he was made a councillor, and in that capacity he was for eight months a State Inquisitor. Having thus attained this diabolically-eminent, or eminently-diabolical, position, he had not much difficulty in shewing his colleagues the necessity of putting me under The Leads as a disturber of the peace of the Republic. In the beginning of the winter the astounding news of the treaty between France and Austria was divulged—a treaty by which the political balance was entirely readjusted, and which was received with incredulity by the Powers. The whole of Italy had reason to rejoice, for the treaty guarded that fair land from becoming the theatre of war on the slightest difference which might arise between the two Powers. What astonished the most acute was that this wonderful treaty was conceived and carried out by a young ambassador who had hitherto been famed only as a wit. The first foundations had been laid in 1750 by Madame de Pompadour, Count Canes (who was created a prince), and M. l'Abbe de Bernis, who was not known till the following year, when the king made him ambassador to Venice. The House of Bourbon and the House of Hapsburg had been foes for two hundred and forty years when this famous treaty was concluded, but it only lasted for forty years, and it is not likely that any treaty will last longer between two courts so essentially opposed to one another.

The Abbe de Bernis was created minister for foreign affairs some time after the ratification of the treaty; three years after he re-established the parliament, became a cardinal, was disgraced, and finally sent to Rome, where he died. 'Mors ultimo linea rerum est'.

Affairs fell out as I had foreseen, for nine months after he left Venice he conveyed to M——M——the news of his recall, though he did it in the most delicate manner. Nevertheless, M——M——felt the blow so severely that she would very possibly have succumbed, had I not been preparing her for it in every way I could think of M. de Bernis sent me all instructions.

He directed that all the contents of the casino should be sold and the proceeds given to M—— M——, with the exception of the books and prints which the housekeeper was ordered to bring to Paris. It was a nice breviary for a cardinal, but would to God they had nothing worse!

Whilst M—— M—— abandoned herself to grief I carried out the orders of M. de Bernis, and by the middle of January we had no longer a casino. She kept by her two thousand sequins and her pearls, intending to sell them later on to buy herself an annuity.

We were now only able to see each other at the grating; and soon, worn with grief, she fell dangerously ill, and on the 2nd of February I recognized in her features the symptoms of approaching death. She sent me her jewel-case, with all her diamonds and nearly all her money, all the scandalous books she possessed, and all her letters, telling me that if she did not die I was to return her the whole, but that all belonged to me if, as she thought, she should succumb to the disease. She also told me that C—— C——was aware of her state, and asked me to take pity on her and write to her, as my letters were her only comfort, and that she hoped to have strength to read them till her latest breath.

I burst into tears, for I loved her passionately, and I promised her to come and live in Muran until she recovered her health.

Having placed the property in a gondola, I went to the Bragadin Palace to deposit it, and then returned to Muran to get Laura to find me a furnished room where I could live as I liked. "I know of a good room, with meals provided," she said; "you will be quite comfortable and will get it cheaply, and if you like to pay in advance, you need not even say who you are. The old man to whom the house belongs lives on the ground floor; he will give you all the keys and if you like you need see no one."

She gave me the address, and I went there on the spot, and having found everything to my liking I paid a month in advance and the thing was done. It was a little house at the end of a blind alley abutting on the canal. I returned to Laura's house to tell her that I wanted a servant to get my food and to make my bed, and she promised to get me one by the next day.

Having set all in order for my new lodging, I returned to Venice and packed my mails as if I were about to make a long journey. After supper I took leave of M. de Bragadin and of his two friends, telling them that I was going to be away for several weeks on important business.

Next day, going to my new room, I was surprised to find there Tonine, Laura's daughter, a pretty girl not more than fifteen years old, who told me with a blush, but with more spirit than I gave her credit for, that she would serve me as well as her mother would have done.

I was in too much distress to thank Laura for this pretty present, and I even determined that her daughter should not stay in my service. We know how much such resolutions are commonly worth. In the meanwhile I was kind to the girl: "I am sure," I said, "of your goodwill, but I must talk to your mother. I must be alone," I added, "as I have to write all day, and I shall not take anything till the evening." She then gave me a letter, begging pardon for not having given it me sooner. "You must never forget to deliver messages," I said, "for if you had waited any longer before bringing me this letter, it might have had the most serious consequences." She blushed, begged pardon, and went out of the room. The letter was from C—— C——, who told me that her friend was in bed, and that the doctor had pronounced her illness to be fever. I passed the rest of the day in putting my room in order, and in writing to C—— C—— and her suffering friend.

Towards evening Tonine brought in the candles, and told me that my supper was ready. "Follow me," I said. Seeing that she had only laid supper for one—a pleasing proof of her modesty, I told her to get another knife and fork, as I wished her always to take her meals with me. I can give no account of my motives. I only wished to be kind to her, and I did everything in good faith. By and by, reader, we shall see whether this is not one of the devices by which the devil compasses his ends.

Not having any appetite, I ate little, but I thought everything good with the exception of the wine; but Tonine promised to get some better by the next day, and when supper was over she went to sleep in the ante-room.

After sealing my letters, wishing to know whether the outer door was locked, I went out and saw Tonine in bed, sleeping peacefully, or pretending to do so. I might have suspected her thoughts, but I had never been in a similar situation, and I measured the extremity of my grief by the indifference with which I looked at this girl; she was pretty, but for all that I felt that neither she nor I ran any risk.

Next day, waking very early, I called her, and she came in neatly dressed. I gave her my letter to C—— C——, which enclosed the letter to M—— M——, telling her to take it to her mother and then to return to make my coffee.

"I shall dine at noon, Tonine," I said, "take care to get what is necessary in good time."

"Sir, I prepared yesterday's supper myself, and if you like I can cook all your meals."

"I am satisfied with your abilities, go on, and here is a sequin for expenses."

"I still have a hundred and twenty sous remaining from the one you gave me yesterday, and that will be enough."

"No, they are for yourself, and I shall give you as much every day."

Her delight was so great that I could not prevent her covering my hand with kisses. I took care to draw it back and not to kiss her in return, for I felt as if I should be obliged to laugh, and this would have dishonoured my grief.

The second day passed like the first. Tonine was glad that I said no more about speaking to her mother, and drew the conclusion that her services were agreeable to me. Feeling tired and weak, and fearing that I should not wake early enough to send the letter to the convent, but not wishing to rouse Tonine if she were asleep, I called her softly. She rose immediately and came into my room with nothing on but a slight petticoat. Pretending to see nothing, I gave her my letter, and told her to take it to her mother in the morning before she came into my room. She went out, saying that my instructions should be carried out, but as soon as she was gone I could not resist saying to myself that she was very pretty; and I felt both sad and ashamed at the reflection that this girl could very easily console me. I hugged my grief, and I determined to separate myself from a being who made me forget it.

"In the morning," I said, "I will tell Laura to get me something less seducing;" but the night brought counsel, and in the morning I put on the armour of sophism, telling myself that my weakness was no fault of the girl's, and that it would therefore be unjust to punish her for it. We shall see, dear reader, how all this ended.

III

Tontine had what is called tact and common sense, and thinking these qualities were required in our economy she behaved with great delicacy, not going to bed before receiving my letters, and never coming into my room except in a proper dress, and all this pleased me. For a fortnight M—— M—— was so ill that I expected every moment to hear the news of her death. On Shrove Tuesday C—— C—— wrote that her friend was not strong enough to read my letter, and that she was going to receive 'extreme unction'. This news so shocked me that I could not rise, and passed the whole day in weeping and writing, Tonine not leaving me till midnight. I could not sleep. On Ash Wednesday I got a letter, in which C—— C—— told me that the doctor had no hopes for her friend, and that he only gave her a fortnight to live. A low fever was wasting her away, her weakness was extreme, and she could scarcely swallow a little broth. She had also the misfortune to be harassed by her confessor, who made her foretaste all the terrors of death. I could only solace my grief by writing, and Tonine now and again made bold to observe that I was cherishing my grief, and that it would be the death of me. I knew myself that I was making my anguish more poignant, and that keeping to my bed, continued writing, and no food, would finally drive me mad. I had told my grief to poor Tonine, whose chief duty was to wipe away my tears. She had compassion on me.

A few days later, after assuring C—— C—— that if our friend died I should not survive her, I asked her to tell M—— M—— that if she wanted me to take care of my life she must promise to let me carry her off on her recovery.

"I have," I said, "four thousand sequins and her diamonds, which are worth six thousand; we should, therefore, have a sufficient sum to enable us to live honourably in any part of Europe."

C—— C—— wrote to me on the following day, and said that my mistress, after hearing my letter read, had fallen into a kind of convulsion, and, becoming delirious, she talked incessantly in French for three whole hours in a fashion which would have made all the nuns take to their heels, if they had understood her. I was in despair, and was nearly raving as wildly as my poor nun. Her delirium lasted three days, and as soon as she got back her reason she charged her young friend to tell me that she was sure to get well if I promised to keep to my word, and to carry her off as soon as her health would allow. I hastened to reply that if I lived she might be sure my promise would be fulfilled.

Thus continuing to deceive each other in all good faith, we got better, for every letter from C—— C——, telling me how the convalescence of her friend was progressing, was to me as balm. And as my mind grew more composed my appetite also grew better, and my health improving day by day, I soon, though quite unconsciously, began to take pleasure in the simple ways of Tonine, who now never left me at night before she saw that I was asleep.

Towards the end of March M——M——wrote to me herself, saying that she believed herself out of danger, and that by taking care she hoped to be able to leave her room after Easter. I replied that I should not leave Muran till I had the pleasure of seeing her at the grating, where, without hurrying ourselves, we could plan the execution of our scheme.

It was now seven weeks since M. de Bragadin had seen me, and thinking that he would be getting anxious I resolved to go and see him that very day. Telling Tonine that I should not be back till the evening, I started for Venice without a cloak, for having gone to Muran masked I had forgotten to take one. I had spent forty-eight days without going out of my room, chiefly in tears and distress, and without taking any food. I had just gone through an experience which flattered my self-esteem. I had been served by a girl who would have passed for a beauty anywhere in Europe. She was gentle, thoughtful, and delicate, and without being taxed with foppishness I think I may say that, if she was not in love with me, she was at all events inclined to please me to the utmost of her ability; for all that I had been able to withstand her youthful charms, and I now scarcely dreaded them. Seeing her every day, I had dispersed my amorous fancies, and friendship and gratitude seemed to have vanquished all other feelings, for I was obliged to confess that this charming girl had lavished on me the most tender and assiduous care.

She had passed whole nights on a chair by my bedside, tending me like a mother, and never giving me the slightest cause for complaint.

Never had I given her a kiss, never had I allowed myself to undress in her presence, and never (with one exception) had she come into my room without being properly dressed. For all that, I knew that I had fought a battle, and I felt inclined to boast at having won the victory. There was only one circumstance that vexed me—namely, that I was nearly certain that neither M. M. nor C. C. would consider such continence to be within the bounds of possibility, if they heard of it, and that Laura herself, to whom her daughter would tell the whole story, would be sceptical, though she might out of kindness pretend to believe it all.

I got to M. de Bragadin's just as the soup was being served. He welcomed me heartily, and was delighted at having foreseen that I should thus surprise them. Besides my two other old friends, there were De la Haye, Bavois, and Dr. Righelini at table.

"What! you without a cloak!" said M. Dandolo.

"Yes," said I; "for having gone out with my mask on I forgot to bring one."

At this they laughed, and, without putting myself out, I sat down. No one asked where I had been so long, for it was understood that that question should be left to me to answer or not. Nevertheless, De la Haye, who was bursting with curiosity, could not refrain from breaking some jests on me.

"You have got so thin," said he, "that uncharitable people will be rather hard on you."

"I trust they will not say that I have been passing my time with the Jesuits."

"You are sarcastic. They may say, perhaps, that you have passed your time in a hot-house under the influence of Mercury."

"Don't be afraid, sir, for to escape this hasty judgment I shall go back this evening."

"No, no, I am quite sure you will not."

"Believe me, sir," said I, with a bantering tone, "that I deem your opinion of too much consequence not to be governed by it."

Seeing that I was in earnest, my friends were angry with him; and the Aristarchus was in some confusion.

Righelini, who was one of Murray's intimate friends, said to me in a friendly way that he had been longing to tell Murray of my reappearance, and of the falsity of all the reports about me.

"We will go to sup with him," said I, "and I will return after supper."

Seeing that M. de Bragadin and his two friends were uneasy about me, I promised to dine with them on April 25th, St. Mark's Day.

As soon as Mr. Murray saw me, he fell on my neck and embraced me. He introduced me to his wife, who asked me to supper with great politeness. After Murray had told me the innumerable stories which had been made about my disappearance, he asked me if I knew a little story by the Abbe Chiari, which had come out at the end of the carnival. As I said that I knew nothing about it, he gave me a copy, telling me that I should like it. He was right. It was a satire in which the Zorzi clique was pulled to pieces, and in which I played a very poor part. I did not read it till some time after, and in the mean time put it in my pocket. After a very good supper I took a gondola to return to Muran.

It was midnight and very dark, so that I did not perceive the gondola to be ill covered and in wretched order. A fine rain was falling when I got in, and the drops getting larger I was soon wet to the skin. No great harm was done, as I was close to my quarters. I groped my way upstairs and knocked at the door of the ante-room, where Tonine, who had not waited for me, was sleeping. Awake in a moment she came to open the door in her smock, and without a light. As I wanted one, I told her to get the flint and steel, which she did, warning me in a modest voice that she was not dressed. "That's of no consequence," said I, "provided you are covered." She said no more, and soon lighted a candle, but she could not help laughing when she saw me dripping wet.

"I only want you, my dear," said I, "to dry my hair." She quickly set to work with powder and powder-puff in hand, but her smock was short and loose at the top, and I repented, rather too late, that I had not given her time to dress. I felt that all was lost, all the more as having to use both her hands she could not hold her smock and conceal two swelling spheres more seductive than the apples of the Hesperides. How could I help seeing them? I shut my eyes and, said "For shame!" but I gave in at last, and fixed such a hungry gaze upon poor Tonine that she blushed. "Come," said I, "take your smock between your teeth and then I shall see no more." But it was worse than before, and I had only added fuel to the fire; for, as the veil was short, I could see the bases and almost the frieze of two marble columns; and at this sight I gave a voluptuous cry. Not knowing how to conceal everything from my gaze, Tonine let herself fall on the sofa, and I, my passions at fever-heat, stood beside her, not knowing what to do.

"Well," she said, "shall I go and dress myself and then do your hair?"

"No, come and sit on my knee, and cover my eyes with your hands."
She came obediently, but the die was cast, and my resistance overcome.
I clasped her between my arms, and without any more thoughts of
playing at blind man's buff I threw her on the bed and covered her with
kisses. And as I swore that I would always love her, she opened her arms
to receive me in a way that shewed how long she had been waiting for
this moment.

I plucked the rose, and then, as ever, I thought it the rarest I had
ever gathered since I had laboured in the harvest of the fruitful fields
of love.

When I awoke in the morning I found myself more deeply in love
with Tonine than I had been with any other woman. She had got up
without waking me, but as soon as she heard me stirring she came, and
I tenderly chid her for not waiting for me to give her good morrow.
Without answering she gave me M—— M——'s letter. I thanked her,
but putting the letter on one side I took her in my arms, and set her
by my side. "What a wonder!" cried Tonine. "You are not in a hurry
to read that letter! Faithless man, why did you not let me cure you six
weeks ago. How lucky I am; thanks to the rain! I do not blame you, dear,
but love me as you love her who writes to you every day, and I shall be
satisfied."

"Do you know who she is?"

"She lives in a boarding-house, and is as beautiful as an angel; but she
is there, and I am here. You are my master, and I will be your servant as
long as you like."

I was glad to leave her in error, and swore an ever-lasting love; but
during our conversation she had let herself drop down in the bottom of
the bed, and I entreated her to lie down again; but she said that on the
contrary it was time for me to get up for dinner, for she wanted to give
me a dainty meal cooked in the Venetian manner.

"Who is the cook?" said I.

"I am, and I have been using all my skill on it since five, when I
got up."

"What time is it now, then?"

"Past one."

The girl astonished me. She was no longer the shy Tonine of last
night; she had that exultant air which happiness bestows, and the look
of pleasure which the delights of love give to a young beauty. I could not
understand how I had escaped from doing homage to her beauty when

I first saw her at her mother's house. But I was then too deeply in love with C——— C———; I was in too great distress; and, moreover, Tonine was then unformed. I got up, and making her bring me a cup of coffee I asked her to keep the dinner back for a couple of hours.

I found M——— M———'s letter affectionate, but not so interesting as it would have been the day before. I set myself to answer it, and was almost thunderstruck to find the task, for the first time, a painful one. However, my short journey to Venice supplied me with talk which covered four pages.

I had an exquisite dinner with my charming Tonine. Looking at her as at the same time my wife, my mistress, and my housekeeper, I was delighted to find myself made happy at such a cheap rate. We spent the whole day at the table talking of our love, and giving each other a thousand little marks of it; for there is no such rich and pleasant matter for conversation as when they who talk are parties to an amorous suit. She told with charming simplicity that she knew perfectly well that she could not make me amorous of her, because I loved another, and that her only hope was therefore in a surprise, and that she had foreseen the happy moment when I told her that she need not dress herself to light a candle.

Tonine was naturally quick-witted, but she did not know either how to read or to write. She was enchanted to see herself become rich (for she thought herself so) without a soul at Muran being able to breathe a word against her honour. I passed three weeks in the company of this delightful girl—weeks which I still reckon among the happiest of my life; and what embitters my old age is that, having a heart as warm as ever, I have no longer the strength necessary to secure a single day as blissful as those which I owed to this charming girl.

Towards the end of April I saw M. M. at the grating, looking thin and much changed, but out of danger. I therefore returned to Venice. In my interview, calling my attachment and tender feelings to my aid, I succeeded in behaving myself in such wise that she could not possibly detect the change which a new love had worked in my heart. I shall be, I trust, easily believed when I say that I was not imprudent enough to let her suspect that I had given up the idea of escaping with her, upon which she counted more than ever. I was afraid lest she should fall ill again, if I took this hope away from her. I kept my casino, which cost me little, and as I went to see M. M. twice a week I slept there on those occasions, and made love with my dashing Tonine.

Having kept my word with my friends by dining with them on St. Mark's Day, I went with Dr. Righelini to the parlour of the Vierges to see the taking of the veil.

The Convent of the Vierges is within the jurisdiction of the Doge, whom the nuns style "Most Serene Father." They all belong to the first families in Venice.

While I was praising the beauty of Mother M—— E—— to Dr. Righelini, he whispered to me that he could get her me for a money payment, if I were curious in the matter. A hundred sequins for her and ten sequins for the go-between was the price fixed on. He assured me that Murray had had her, and could have her again. Seeing my surprise, he added that there was not a nun whom one could not have by paying for her: that Murray had the courage to disburse five hundred sequins for a nun of Muran—a rare beauty, who was afterwards the mistress of the French ambassador.

Though my passion for M—— M—— was on the wane, I felt my heart gripped as by a hand of ice, and it was with the greatest difficulty that I made no sign. Notwithstanding, I took the story for an atrocious calumny, but yet the matter was too near my heart for me to delay in bringing it to light at the earliest opportunity. I therefore replied to Righelini in the calmest manner possible, that one or two nuns might be had for money, but that it could happen very rarely on account of the difficulties in most convents.

"As for the nun of Muran, justly famous for her beauty, if she be M—— M——, nun of the convent. . . , I not only disbelieve that Murray ever had her, but I am sure she was never the French ambassador's mistress. If he knew her it could only have been at the grating, where I really cannot say what happens."

Righelini, who was an honourable and spirited man, answered me coldly that the English ambassador was a man of his word, and that he had the story from his own lips.

"If Mr. Murray," he continued, "had not told it me under the seal of secrecy I would make him tell it you himself. I shall be obliged if you will take care that he never knows I told you of it."

"You may rely on my discretion."

The same evening, supping at Murray's casino with Righelini, having the matter at heart, and seeing before me the two men who could clear up everything to my satisfaction, I began to speak with enthusiasm of the beauty of M—— E——, whom I had seen at the Vierges.

Here the ambassador struck in, taking the ball on the hop:

"Between friends," said he, "you can get yourself the enjoyment of those charms, if you are willing to sacrifice a sum of money—not too much, either, but you must have the key."

"Do you think you have it?"

"No, I am sure; and had less trouble than you might suppose."

"If you are sure; I congratulate you, and doubt no more. I envy your fortune, for I don't believe a more perfect beauty could be found in all the convents of Venice."

"There you are wrong. Mother M—— M——, at—— in Muran, is certainly handsomer."

"I have heard her talked of and I have seen her once, but I do not think it possible that she can be procured for money."

"I think so," said he, laughing, "and when I think I mostly have good reasons."

"You surprise me; but all the same I don't mind betting you are deceived."

"You would lose. As you have only seen her once, I suppose you would not recognize her portrait?"

"I should, indeed, as her face left a strong impression on my mind."

"Wait a minute."

He got up from the table, went out, and returned a minute after with a box containing eight or ten miniatures, all in the same style, namely, with hair in disorder and bare necks.

"These," said I, "are rare charms, with which you have doubtless a near acquaintance?"

"Yes, and if you recognize any of them be discreet."

"You need not be afraid. Here are three I recognize, and this looks like M—— M——; but confess that you may have been deceived—at least, that you did not have her in the convent or here, for there are women like her."

"Why do you think I have been deceived? I have had her here in her religious habit, and I have spent a whole night with her; and it was to her individually that I sent a purse containing five hundred sequins. I gave fifty to the good procurer."

"You have, I suppose, visited her in the parlour, after having her here?"

"No, never, as she was afraid her titular lover might hear of it. You know that was the French ambassador."

"But she only saw him in the parlour."

"She used to go to his house in secular dress whenever he wanted her. I was told that by the man who brought her here."

"Have you had her several times?"

"Only once and that was enough, but I can have her whenever I like for a hundred sequins."

"All that may be the truth, but I would wager five hundred sequins that you have been deceived."

"You shall have your answer in three days."

I was perfectly certain, I repeat, that the whole affair was a piece of knavery; but it was necessary to have it proved, and I shuddered when the thought came into my head that after all it might be a true story. In this case I should have been freed from a good many obligations, but I was strongly persuaded of her innocence. At all events, if I were to find her guilty (which was amongst possible occurrences), I resigned myself to lose five hundred sequins as the price of this horrible discovery and addition to my experience of life. I was full of restless anguish—the worst, perhaps, of the torments of the mind. If the honest Englishman had been the victim of a mystification, or rather knavery, my regard for M—— M——'s honour compelled me to find a way to undeceive him without compromising her; and such was my plan, and thus fortune favoured me. Three or four days after, Mr. Murray told the doctor that he wished to see me. We went to him, and he greeted me thus:

"I have won; for a hundred sequins I can have the fair nun!

"Alas!" said I, "there go my five hundred sequins."

"No, not five hundred, my dear fellow, for I should be ashamed to win so much of you, but the hundred she would cost me. If I win, you shall pay for my pleasure, and if I lose I shall give her nothing."

"How is the problem to be solved?" "My Mercury tells me that we must wait for a day when masks are worn. He is endeavouring at present to find out a way to convince both of us; for otherwise neither you nor I would feel compelled to pay the wager, and if I really have M. M. my honour would not allow me to let her suspect that I had betrayed the secret."

"No, that would be an unpardonable crime. Hear my plan, which will satisfy us both; for after it has been carried out each of us will be sure that he has fairly won or fairly lost.

"As soon as you have possessed yourself of the real or pretended nun, leave her on some pretext, and meet me in a place to be agreed upon. We will then go together to the convent, and I will ask for M. M.

"Will seeing her and speaking to her convince you that the woman you have left at home is a mere impostor?"

"Perfectly, and I shall pay my wager with the greatest willingness."

"I may say the same. If, when I summon M. M. to the parlour, the lay-sister tells us she is ill or busy, we will go, and the wager will be yours; you will sup with the fair, and I will go elsewhere."

"So be it; but since all this will be at nighttime, it is possible that when you ask for her, the sister will tell you that no one can be seen at such an hour."

"Then I shall lose."

"You are quite sure, then, that if she be in the convent she will come down?"

"That's my business. I repeat, if you don't speak to her, I shall hold myself to have lost a hundred sequins, or a thousand if you like."

"One can't speak plainer than that, my dear fellow, and I thank you beforehand."

"The only thing I ask you is to come sharp to time; and not to come too late for a convent."

"Will an hour after sunset suit you?"

"Admirably."

"I shall also make it my business to compel my masked mistress to stop where she is, even though it be M. M. herself."

"Some won't have long to wait, if you will take her to a casino which I myself possess at Muran, and where I secretly keep a girl of whom I am amorous. I will take care that she shall not be there on the appointed day, and I will give you the key of the casino. I shall also see that you find a delicate cold supper ready."

"That is admirable, but I must be able to point out the place to my Mercury."

"True! I will give you a supper to-morrow, the greatest secrecy to be observed between us. We will go to my casino in a gondola, and after supper we will go out by the street door; thus you will know the way by land and water. You will only have to tell the procurer the name of the canal and of the house, and on the day fixed you shall have the key. You will only find there an old man who lives on the ground floor, and he will see neither those who go out nor those who come in. My sweetheart will see nothing and will not be seen; and all, trust me, will turn out well."

"I begin to think that I have lost my bet," said the Englishman, who was delighted with the plan; "but it matters not, I can gaily encounter either loss or gain." We made our appointment for the next day, and separated.

On the following morning I went to Muran to warn Tonine that I was going to sup with her, and to bring two of my friends; and as my English friend paid as great court to Bacchus as to Cupid, I took care to send my little housekeeper several bottles of excellent wine.

Charmed with the prospect of doing the honours of the table, Tonine only asked me if my friends would go away after supper. I said yes, and this reply made her happy; she only cared for the dessert.

After leaving her I went to the convent and passed an hour with M. M. in the parlour. I was glad to see that she was getting back her health and her beauty every day, and having complimented her upon it I returned to Venice. In the evening my two friends kept their appointments to the minute, and we went to my little casino at two hours after sunset.

Our supper was delicious, and my Tonine charmed me with the gracefulness of her carriage. I was delighted to see Righelini enchanted, and the ambassador dumb with admiration. When I was in love I did not encourage my friends to cajole my sweetheart, but I became full of complaisance when time had cooled the heat of my passion.

We parted about midnight, and having taken Mr. Murray to the spot where I was to wait for him on the day of trial, I returned to compliment my charming Tonine as she deserved. She praised my two friends, and could not express her surprise at seeing our English friend going away, fresh and nimble on his feet, notwithstanding his having emptied by himself six bottles of my best wine. Murray looked like a fine Bacchus after Rubens.

On Whit Sunday Righelini came to tell me that the English ambassador had made all arrangements with the pretended procurer of M. M. for Whit Tuesday. I gave him the keys of my abode at Muran, and told him to assure Murray that I would keep the appointment at the exact time arranged upon.

My impatience brought on palpitation of the heart, which was extremely painful, and I passed the two nights without closing an eye; for although I was convinced of M——M——'s innocence, my agitation was extreme. But whence all this anxiety? Merely from a desire to see the ambassador undeceived. M. M. must in his eyes have seemed a common prostitute, and the moment in which he would be obliged to confess himself the victim of roguery would re-establish the honour of the nun.

Mr. Murray was as impatient as myself, with this difference, that whereas he, looking upon the adventure as a comic one, only laughed, I who found it too tragic shuddered with indignation.

On Tuesday morning I went to Muran to tell Tonine to get a cold supper after my instruction, to lay the table for two, to get wax lights ready, and having sent in several bottles of wine I bade her keep to the room occupied by the old landlord, and not to come out till the people who were coming in the evening were gone. She promised to do so, and asked no questions. After leaving her I went to the convent parlour, and asked to see M—— M——. Not expecting to see me, she asked me why I had not gone to the pageant of the Bucentaur, which, the weather being favourable, would set out on this day. I do not know what I answered, but I know that she found my words little to the purpose. I came at last to the important point, and told her I was going to ask a favour of her, on which my peace of mind depended, but which she must grant blindly without asking any questions.

"Tell me what I am to do, sweetheart," said she, "and be sure I will refuse nothing which may be in my power."

"I shall be here this evening an hour after sunset, and ask for you at this grating; come. I shall be with another man, to whom I beg of you to say a few words of politeness; you can then leave us. Let us find some pretext to justify the unseasonable hour."

"I will do what you ask, but you cannot imagine how troublesome it is in a convent, for at six o'clock the parlours are shut up and the keys are taken to the abbess' room. However, as you only want me for five minutes, I will tell the abbess that I am expecting a letter from my brother, and that it can be sent to me on this evening only. You must give me a letter that the nun who will be with me may be able to say that I have not been guilty of deception."

"You will not come alone, then?"

"I should not dare even to ask for such a privilege."

"Very good, but try to come with some old nun who is short-sighted."

"I will keep the light in the background."

"Pray do not do so, my beloved; on the contrary, place it so that you may be distinctly seen."

"All this is very strange, but I have promised passive obedience, and I will come down with two lights. May I hope that you will explain this riddle to me at your next interview?"

"By to-morrow, at latest, you shall know the whole story."

"My curiosity will prevent me from sleeping."

"Not so, dear heart; sleep peacefully, and be sure of my gratitude."

The reader will think that after this conversation my heart was perfectly at rest; but how far was I from resting! I returned to Venice, tortured lest I should be told in the evening at the door of the cathedral, where we were to meet, that the nun had been obliged to put off her appointment. If that had happened, I should not have exactly suspected M—— M——, but the ambassador would have thought that I had caused the scheme to miscarry. It is certain that in that case I should not have taken my man to the parlour, but should have gone there sadly by myself.

I passed the whole day in these torments, thinking it would never come to an end, and in the evening I put a letter in my pocket, and went to my post at the hour agreed upon.

Fortunately, Murray kept the appointment exactly.

"Is the nun there?" said I, as soon as he was near me.

"Yes, my dear fellow. We will go, if you like, to the parlour; but you will find that we shall be told she is ill or engaged. If you like, the bet shall be off."

"God forbid, my dear fellow! I cling to that hundred ducats. Let us be gone."

We presented ourselves at the wicket, and I asked for M—— M——, and the doorkeeper made me breathe again by saying that I was expected. I entered the parlour with my English friend, and saw that it was lighted by four candles. I cannot recall these moments without being in love with life. I take note not only of my noble mistress's innocence, but also of the quickness of her wit. Murray remained serious, without a smile on his face. Full of grace and beauty, M—— M—— came into the room with a lay-sister, each of them holding a candlestick. She paid me a compliment in good French; I gave her the letter, and looking at the address and the seal she put it in her pocket. After thanking me and saying she would reply in due course, she turned towards my companion:

"I shall, perhaps, make you lose the first act of the opera," said she.

"The pleasure of seeing you, madam, is worth all the operas in the world."

"You are English, I think?"

"Yes, madam."

"The English are now the greatest people in the world, because they are free and powerful. Gentlemen, I wish you a very good evening."

I had never seen M—— M—— looking so beautiful as then, and I went out of the parlour ablaze with love, and glad as I had never been before. I walked with long strides towards my casino, without taking notice of the ambassador, who did not hurry himself in following me; I waited for him at my door.

"Well," said I, "are you convinced now that you have been cheated?"

"Be quiet, we have time enough to talk about that. Let us go upstairs."

"Shall I come?"

"Do. What do you think I could do by myself for four hours with that creature who is waiting for me? We will amuse ourselves with her."

"Had we not better turn her out?"

"No; her master is coming for her at two o'clock in the morning. She would go and warn him, and he would escape my vengeance. We will throw them both out of the window."

"Be moderate, for M—— M—— s honour depends on the secrecy we observe. Let us go upstairs. We shall have some fun. I should like to see the hussy."

Murray was the first to enter the room. As soon as the girl saw me, she threw her handkerchief over her face, and told the ambassador that such behaviour was unworthy of him. He made no answer. She was not so tall as M—— M——, and she spoke bad French.

Her cloak and mask were on the bed, but she was dressed as a nun. As I wanted to see her face, I politely asked her to do me the favour of shewing it.

"I don't know you," said she; "who are you?"

"You are in my house, and don't know who I am?"

"I am in your house because I have been betrayed. I did not think that I should have to do with a scoundrel."

At this word Murray commanded her to be silent, calling her by the name of her honourable business; and the slut got up to take her cloak, saying she would go. Murray pushed her back, and told her that she would have to wait for her worthy friend, warning her to make no noise if she wanted to keep out of prison.

"Put me in prison!"

With this she directed her hand towards her dress, but I rushed forward and seized one hand while Murray mastered the other. We pushed her back on a chair while we possessed ourselves of the pistols she carried in her pockets.

Murray tore away the front of her holy habit, and I extracted a stiletto eight inches long, the false nun weeping bitterly all the time.

"Will you hold your tongue, and keep quiet till Capsucefalo comes," said the ambassador, "or go to prison?"

"If I keep quiet what will become of me?"

"I promise to let you go."

"With him?"

"Perhaps."

"Very well, then, I will keep quiet."

"Have you got any more weapons?"

Hereupon the slut took off her habit and her petticoat, and if we had allowed her she would have soon been in a state of nature, no doubt in the expectation of our passions granting what our reason refused. I was much astonished to find in her only a false resemblance to M.M. I remarked as much to the ambassador, who agreed with me, but made me confess that most men, prepossessed with the idea that they were going to see M. M., would have fallen into the same trap. In fact, the longing to possess one's self of a nun who has renounced all the pleasures of the world, and especially that of cohabitation with the other sex, is the very apple of Eve, and is more delightful from the very difficulty of penetrating the convent grating.

Few of my readers will fail to testify that the sweetest pleasures are those which are hardest to be won, and that the prize, to obtain which one would risk one's life, would often pass unnoticed if it were freely offered without difficulty or hazard.

In the following chapter, dear reader, you will see the end of this farcical adventure. In the mean time, let us take a little breath.

IV

PLEASANT ENDING OF THE ADVENTURE OF THE FALSE NUN—
M. M. FINDS OUT THAT I HAVE A MISTRESS—SHE IS AVENGED
ON THE WRETCH CAPSUCEFALO—I RUIN MYSELF AT PLAY, AND
AT THE SUGGESTION OF M. M. I SELL ALL HER DIAMONDS,
ONE AFTER ANOTHER—I HAND OVER TONINE TO MURRAY,
WHO MAKES PROVISION FOR HER—HER SISTER BARBERINE
TAKES HER PLACE

How did you make this nice acquaintance?" I asked the ambassador. "Six months ago," he replied, "while standing at the convent gate with Mr. Smith, our consul, in whose company I had been to see some ceremony or other, I remarked to him, as we were talking over some nuns we had noticed, 'I would gladly give five hundred sequins for a few hours of Sister M—— M—— s company.' Count Capsucefalo heard what I said, but made no remark. Mr. Smith answered that one could only see her at the grating as did the ambassador of France, who often came to visit her. Capsucefalo called on me the next morning, and said that if I had spoken in good faith he was sure he could get me a night with the nun in whatever place I liked, if she could count on my secrecy. 'I have just been speaking to her,' said he, 'and on my mentioning your name she said she had noticed you with Mr. Smith, and vowed she would sup with you more for love than money. 'I,' said the rascal, 'am the only man she trusts, and I take her to the French ambassador's casino in Venice whenever she wants to go there. You need not be afraid of being cheated, as you will give the money to her personally when you have possessed yourself of her.' With this he took her portrait from his pocket and shewed it me; and here it is. I bought it of him two days after I believed myself to have spent a night with the charming nun, and a fortnight after our conversation. This beauty here came masked in a nun's habit, and I was fool enough to think I had got a treasure. I am vexed with myself for not having suspected the cheat—at all events, when I saw her hair, as I know that nuns' hair should be cut short. But when I said something about it to the hussy, she told me they were allowed to keep their hair under their caps, and I was weak enough to believe her."

I knew that on this particular Murray had not been deceived, but I did not feel compelled to tell him so then and there.

I held the portrait Murray had given me in my hand, and compared it with the face before me. In the portrait the breast was bare, and as I was remarking that painters did those parts as best they could, the impudent wench seized the opportunity to shew me that the miniature was faithful to nature. I turned my back upon her with an expression of contempt which would have mortified her, if these creatures were ever capable of shame. As we talked things over, I could not help laughing at the axiom, Things which are equal to the same thing are equal to one another, for the miniature was like M. M. and like the courtezan, and yet the two women were not like each other. Murray agreed with me, and we spent an hour in a philosophical discussion on the matter. As the false M. M. was named Innocente, we expressed a wish to know how her name agreed with her profession, and how the knave had induced her to play the part she had taken; and she told us the following story:

"I have known Count Capsucefalo for two years, and have found him useful, for, though he has given me no money, he has made me profit largely through the people he has introduced to me. About the end of last autumn he came to me one day, and said that if I could make up as a nun with some clothes he would get me, and in that character pass a night with an Englishman, I should be the better by five hundred sequins. 'You need not be afraid of anything,' said he, 'as I myself will take you to the casino where the dupe will be awaiting you, and I will come and take you back to your imaginary convent towards the end of the night. He shewed me how I must behave, and told me what to reply if my lover asked any questions about the discipline of the convent.

"I liked the plot, gentlemen, and I told him I was ready to carry it out. And be pleased to consider that there are not many women of my profession who would hesitate over a chance of getting five hundred sequins. Finding the scheme both agreeable and profitable, I promised to play my part with the greatest skill. The bargain was struck, and he gave me full instructions as to my dialogue. He told me that the Englishman could only talk about my convent and any lovers I might have had; that on the latter point I was to cut him short, and to answer with a laugh that I did not know what he was talking about, and even to tell him that I was a nun in appearance only, and that in the course of toying I might let him see my hair. 'That,' said Capsucefalo, 'won't prevent him from thinking you a nun—yes! and the very nun he is amorous of, for he will have made up his mind that you cannot possibly be anyone else.' Seizing the point of the jest, I did not take the trouble to find out the name of the nun I was to represent, nor the convent whence I was to come; the only thing in my head was the five hundred sequins. So little have I troubled about aught else that, though I passed a delicious night with you, and found you rather worthy of being paid for than paying, I have not ascertained who and what you are, and I don't know at this moment to whom I am speaking. You know what a night I had; I have told you it was delicious, and I was happy in the idea that I was going to have another. You have found everything out. I am sorry, but I am not afraid of anything, since I can put on any disguise I like, and can't prevent my lovers taking me for a saint if they like to do so. You have found weapons in my possession, but everyone is allowed to bear arms in self-defence. I plead not guilty on all counts."

"Do you know me?" said I.

"No, but I have often seen you passing under my window. I live at St. Roch, near the bridge."

The way in which the woman told her yarn convinced us that she was an adept in the science of prostitution, but we thought Capsucefalo, in spite of the count, worthy of the pillory. The girl was about ten years older than M. M., she was pretty, but light-complexioned, while my beautiful nun had fine dark brown hair and was at least three inches taller.

After twelve o'clock we sat down to supper, and did honour to the excellent meal which my dear Antoinette had prepared for us. We were cruel enough to leave the poor wretch without offering her so much as a glass of wine, but we thought it our duty.

While we were talking, the jolly Englishman made some witty comments on my eagerness to convince him that he had not enjoyed M. M.'s favours.

"I can't believe," said he, "that you have shewn so much interest without being in love with the divine nun."

I answered by saying that if I were her lover I was much to be pitied in being condemned to go to the parlour, and no farther.

"I would gladly give a hundred guineas a month," said he, "to have the privilege of visiting her at the grating."

So saying he gave me my hundred sequins, complimenting me on my success, and I slipped them forthwith into my pocket.

At two o'clock in the morning we heard a soft knock on the street door.

"Here is our friend," I said, "be discreet, and you will see that he will make a full confession."

He came in and saw Murray and the lady, but did not discover that a third party was present till he heard the ante-room door being locked. He turned round and saw me, and as he knew me, merely said, without losing countenance:

"Ah, you are here; you know, of course, that the secret must be kept?"

Murray laughed and calmly asked him to be seated, and he enquired, with the lady's pistols in his hands, where he was going to take her before day-break.

"Home."

"I think you may be mistaken, as it is very possible that when you leave this place you will both of you be provided with a bed in prison."

"No, I am not afraid of that happening; the thing would make too much noise, and the laugh would not be on your side. Come," said he to his mate, "put on your cloak and let us be off."

The ambassador, who like an Englishman kept quite cool the whole time, poured him out a glass of Chambertin, and the blackguard drank his health. Murray seeing he had on a fine ring set with brilliants, praised it, and shewing some curiosity to see it more closely he drew it off the fellow's finger, examined it, found it without flaw, and asked how much it was worth. Capsucefalo, a little taken aback, said it cost him four hundred sequins.

"I will hold it as a pledge for that sum," said the ambassador, putting the ring into his pocket. The other looked chop-fallen, and Murray laughing at his retiring manners told the girl to put on her cloak and to pack off with her worthy acolyte. She did so directly, and with a low bow they disappeared.

"Farewell, nun procurer!" said the ambassador, but the count made no answer.

As soon as they were gone I thanked Murray warmly for the moderation he had shewn, as a scandal would have only injured three innocent people.

"Be sure," said he, "that the guilty parties shall be punished without anyone's knowing the reason."

I then made Tonine come upstairs, and my English friend offered her a glass of wine, which she declined with much modesty and politeness. Murray looked at her with flaming glances, and left after giving me his heartiest thanks.

Poor little Tonine had been resigned, and obedient for many hours, and she had good cause to think I had been unfaithful to her; however, I gave her the most unmistakable proofs of my fidelity. We stayed in bed for six hours, and rose happy in the morning.

After dinner I hurried off to my noble M—— M——, and told her the whole story. She listened eagerly, her various feelings flitting across her face. Fear, anger, wrath, approval of my method of clearing up my natural suspicions, joy at discovering me still her lover—all were depicted in succession in her glance, and in the play of her features, and in the red and white which followed one another on her cheeks and forehead. She was delighted to hear that the masker who was with me in the parlour was the English ambassador, but she became nobly disdainful when I told her that he would gladly give a hundred guineas a month for the pleasure of visiting her in the parlour. She was angry with him for fancying that she had been in his power, and for finding a likeness between her and a portrait, when, so she said, there was no likeness at all; I had given her the portrait. She added, with a shrewd smile, that she was sure I had not let my little maid see the false nun, as she might have been mistaken.

"You know, do you, that I have a young servant?"

"Yes, and a pretty one, too. She is Laura's daughter, and if you love her I am very glad, and so is C—— C——. I hope you will let me have a sight of her. C—— C—— has seen her before."

As I saw that she knew too much for me to be able to deceive her, I took my cue directly and told her in detail the history of my amours. She shewed her satisfaction too openly not to be sincere. Before I left her she said her honour obliged her to get Capsucefalo assassinated, for the wretch had wronged her beyond pardon. By way of quieting her I promised that if the ambassador did not rid us of him within the week I would charge myself with the execution of our common vengeance.

About this time died Bragadin the procurator, brother of my patron, leaving M. de Bragadin sufficiently well off. However, as the family threatened to become extinct, he desired a woman who had been his mistress, and of whom he had had a natural son, to become his wife. By this marriage the son would have become legitimate, and the family renewed again. The College of Cardinals would have recognized the wife for a small fee, and all would have gone admirably.

The woman wrote to me, asking me to call on her; and I was going to, curious to know what a woman, whom I did not know from Adam, could want with me, when I received a summons from M. de Bragadin. He begged me to ask Paralis if he ought to follow De la Haye's advice in a matter he had promised not to confide to me, but of which the oracle must be informed. The oracle, naturally opposed to the Jesuit, told him to consult his own feelings and nothing else. After this I went to the lady.

She began by telling me the whole story. She introduced her son to me, and told me that if the marriage could be performed, a deed would be delivered in my favour by which, at the death of M. de Bragadin, I should become entitled to an estate worth five thousand crowns per annum.

As I guessed without much trouble that this was the same matter which De la Haye had proposed to M. de Bragadin, I answered without hesitation that since De la Haye was before me I could do nothing, and thereupon made her my bow.

I could not help wondering at this Jesuit's continually intriguing to marry my old friends without my knowledge. Two years ago, if I had not set my face against it, he would have married M. Dandolo. I cared not a whit whether the family of Bragadin became extinct or not, but I did care for the life of my benefactor, and was quite sure that marriage would shorten it by many years; he was already sixty-three, and had recovered from a serious apoplectic stroke.

I went to dine with Lady Murray (English-women who are daughters of lords keep the title), and after dinner the ambassador told me that he had told M. Cavalli the whole story of the false nun, and that the secretary had informed him, the evening before, that everything had been done to his liking. Count Capsucefalo had been sent to Cephalonia, his native country, with the order never to return to Venice, and the courtezan had disappeared.

The fine part, or rather the fearful part, about these sentences is that no one ever knows the reason why or wherefore, and that the lot may fall on the innocent as well as the guilty. M. M. was delighted with the event, and I was more pleased than she, for I should have been sorry to have been obliged to soil my hands with the blood of that rascally count.

There are seasons in the life of men which may be called 'fasti' and 'nefasti'; I have proved this often in my long career, and on the strength of the rubs and struggles I have had to encounter. I am able, as well as any man, to verify the truth of this axiom. I had just experienced a run of luck. Fortune had befriended me at play, I had been happy in the society of men, and from love I had nothing to ask; but now the reverse of the medal began to appear. Love was still kind, but Fortune had quite left me, and you will soon see, reader, that men used me no better than the blind goddess. Nevertheless, since one's fate has phases as well as the moon, good follows evil as disasters succeed to happiness.

I still played on the martingale, but with such bad luck that I was soon left without a sequin. As I shared my property with M. M. I was obliged to tell her of my losses, and it was at her request that I sold all her diamonds, losing what I got for them; she had now only five hundred sequins by her. There was no more talk of her escaping from the convent, for we had nothing to live on! I still gamed, but for small stakes, waiting for the slow return of good luck.

One day the English ambassador, after giving me a supper at his casino with the celebrated Fanny Murray, asked me to let him sup at my casino at Muran, which I now only kept up for the sake of Tonine. I granted him the favour, but did not imitate his generosity. He found my little mistress smiling and polite, but always keeping within the bounds of decency, from which he would have very willingly excused her. The next morning he wrote to me as follows:

"I am madly in love with Tonine. If you like to hand her over to me I will make the following provision for her: I will set her up in a suitable lodging which I will furnish throughout, and which I will give to her with all its contents, provided that I may visit her whenever I please, and that she gives me all the rights of a fortunate lover. I will give her a maid, a cook, and thirty sequins a month as provision for two people, without reckoning the wine, which I will procure myself. Besides this I will give her a life income of two hundred crowns per annum, over which she will have full control after living with me for a year. I give you a week to send your answer."

I replied immediately that I would let him know in three days whether his proposal were accepted, for Tonine had a mother of whom she was fond, and she would possibly not care to do anything without her consent. I also informed him that in all appearance the girl was with child.

The business was an important one for Tonine. I loved her, but I knew perfectly well that we could not pass the rest of our lives together, and I saw no prospect of being able to make her as good a provision as that offered by the ambassador. Consequently I had no doubts on the question, and the very same day I went to Muran and told her all.

"You wish to leave me, then," said she, in tears.

"I love you, dearest, and what I propose ought to convince you of my love."

"Not so; I cannot serve two masters."

"You will only serve your new lover, sweetheart. I beg of you to reflect that you will have a fine dowry, on the strength of which you may marry well; and that however much I love you I cannot possibly make so good a provision for you."

"Leave me to-day for tears and reflection, and come to supper with me to-morrow."

I did not fail to keep the appointment.

"I think your English friend is a very pretty man," she said, "and when he speaks in the Venetian dialect it makes me die with laughter. If my mother agrees, I might, perhaps, force myself to love him. Supposing we did not agree we could part at the end of a year, and I should be the richer by an income of two hundred crowns."

"I am charmed with the sense of your arguments; speak about it to your mother."

"I daren't, sweetheart; this kind of thing is too delicate to be discussed between a mother and her daughter speak to her yourself."

"I will, indeed."

Laura, whom I had not seen since she had given me her daughter, asked for no time to think it over, but full of glee told me that now her daughter would be able to soothe her declining years, and that she would leave Muran of which she was tired. She shewed me a hundred and thirty sequins which Tonine had gained in my service, and which she had placed in her hands.

Barberine, Tonine's younger sister, came to kiss my hand. I thought her charming, and I gave her all the silver in my pocket. I then left, telling Laura that I should expect her at my house. She soon followed me, and gave her child a mother's blessing, telling her that she and her family could go and live in Venice for sixty sous a day. Tonine embraced her, and told her that she should have it.

This important affair having been managed to everybody's satisfaction, I went to see M—— M——, who came into the parlour with C—— C——, whom I found looking sad, though prettier than ever. She was melancholy, but none the less tender. She could not stay for more than a quarter of an hour for fear of being seen, as she was forbidden ever to go into the parlour. I told M. M. the story of Tonine, who was going to live with Murray in Venice; she was sorry to hear it, "for," said she, "now that you have no longer any attraction at Muran, I shall see you less than ever." I promised to come and see her often, but vain promises! The time was near which parted us for ever.

The same evening I went to tell the good news to my friend Murray. He was in a transport of joy, and begged me to come and sup with him at his casino the day after next, and to bring the girl with me, that the surrender might be made in form. I did not fail him, for once the matter was decided, I longed to bring it to an end. In my presence he assigned to her the yearly income for her life of two hundred Venetian ducats, and by a second deed he gave her all the contents of the house with which he was going to provide her, provided always that she lived with him for a year. He allowed her to receive me as a friend, also to receive her mother and sisters, and she was free to go and see them when she would. Tonine threw her arms about his neck, and assured him that she would endeavour to please him to the utmost of her ability. "I will see him," said she, pointing to me, "but as his friend he shall have nothing more from me." Throughout this truly affecting scene she kept back her tears, but I could not conceal mine. Murray was happy, but I was not long a witness of his good fortune, the reason of which I will explain a little later.

Three days afterwards Laura came to me, told me that she was living in Venice, and asked me to take her to her daughter's. I owed this woman too much to refuse her, and I took her there forthwith. Tonine gave thanks to God, and also to me, and her mother took up the song, for they were not quite sure whether they were more indebted to God or to me. Tonine was eloquent in her praise of Murray, and made no complaint at my not having come to see her, at which I was glad. As I was going Laura asked me to take her back in my gondola, and as we had to pass by the house in which she lived she begged me to come in for a moment, and I could not hurt her feelings by refusing. I owe it to my honour to remark here that I was thus polite without thinking that I should see Barberine again.

This girl, as pretty as her sister, though in another style, began by awakening my curiosity—a weakness which usually renders the profligate man inconstant. If all women were to have the same features, the same disposition, and the same manners, men would not only never be inconstant, but would never be in love. Under that state of things one would choose a wife by instinct and keep to her till death, but our world would then be under a different system to the present. Novelty is the master of the soul. We know that what we do not see is very nearly the same as what we have seen, but we are curious, we like to be quite sure, and to attain our ends we give ourselves as much trouble as if we were certain of finding some prize beyond compare.

Barberine, who looked upon me as an old friend—for her mother had accustomed her to kiss my hand whenever I went there, who had undressed more than once in my presence without troubling about me, who knew I had made her sister's fortune and the family fortune as well, and thought herself prettier than Tonine because her skin was fairer, and because she had fine black eyes, desiring to take her sister's place, knew that to succeed she must take me by storm. Her common sense told her that as I hardly ever came to the house, I should not be likely to become amorous of her unless she won me by storm; and to this end she shewed the utmost complaisance when she had the chance, so that I won her without any difficulty. All this reasoning came from her own head, for I am sure her mother gave her no instructions. Laura was a mother of a kind common the world over, but especially in Italy. She was willing to take advantage of the earnings of her daughters, but she would never have induced them to take the path of evil. There her virtue stopped short.

After I had inspected her two rooms and her little kitchen, and had admired the cleanness which shone all around, Barberine asked me if I would like to see their small garden.

"With pleasure," I replied, "for a garden is a rarity in Venice."

Her mother told her to give me some figs if there were any ripe ones. The garden consisted of about thirty square feet, and grew only salad herbs and a fine fig tree. It had not a good crop, and I told her that I could not see any figs.

"I can see some at the top," said Barberine, "and I will gather them if you will hold me the ladder."

"Yes, climb away; I will hold it quite firmly."

She stepped up lightly, and stretching out an arm to get at some figs to one side of her, she put her body off its balance, holding on to the ladder with the other hand.

"My dear Barberine, what do you think I can see?"

"What you have often seen with my sister."

"That's true! but you are prettier than she is."

The girl made no reply, but, as if she could not reach the fruit, she put her foot on a high branch, and spewed me the most seductive picture. I was in an ecstasy, and Barberine, who saw it, did not hurry herself. At last I helped her to come down, and letting my hand wander indiscreetly, I asked her if the fruit I held had been plucked, and she kept me a long time telling me it was quite fresh. I took her within my arms, and already her captive, I pressed her amorously to my heart, printing on her lips a fiery kiss, which she gave me back with as much ardour.

"Will you give me what I have caught, dearest?"

"My mother is going to Muran to-morrow, and she will stay there all the day; if you come, there is nothing I will refuse you."

When speech like this proceeds from a mouth still innocent, the man to whom it is addressed ought to be happy, for desires are but pain and torment, and enjoyment is sweet because it delivers us from them. This shews that those who prefer a little resistance to an easy conquest are in the wrong; but a too easy conquest often points to a depraved nature, and this men do not like, however depraved they themselves may be.

We returned to the house, and I gave Barberine a tender kiss before Laura's eyes, telling her that she had a very jewel in her daughter—a compliment which made her face light up with pleasure. I gave the dear girl ten sequins, and I went away congratulating myself, but cursing my luck at not being able to make as good provision for Barberine as Murray had made for her sister.

Tonine had told me that for manners' sake I should sup once with her. I went the same evening and found Righelini and Murray there. The supper was delicious, and I was delighted with the excellent understanding the two lovers had already come to. I complimented the ambassador on the loss of one of his tastes, and he told me he should be very sorry at such a loss, as it would warn him of his declining powers.

"But," said I, "you used to like to perform the mysterious sacrifice of Love without a veil."

"It was not I but Ancilla who liked it, and as I preferred pleasing her to pleasing myself, I gave in to her taste without any difficulty."

"I am delighted with your answer, as I confess it would cost me something to be the witness of your exploits with Tonine."

Having casually remarked that I had no longer a house in Muran, Righelini told me that if I liked he could get me a delightful house at a low rent on the Tondamente Nuovo.

As this quarter facing north, and as agreeable in summer as disagreeable in winter, was opposite to Muran, where I should have to go twice a week, I told the doctor I should be glad to look at the house.

I took leave of the rich and fortunate ambassador at midnight, and before passing the day with my new prize I went to sleep so as to be fresh and capable of running a good course.

I went to Barberine at an early hour, and as soon as she saw me she said,

"My mother will not be back till the evening, and my brother will take his dinner at the school. Here is a fowl, a ham, some cheese, and two bottles of Scopolo wine. We will take our mess whenever you like:"

"You astonish me, sweetheart, for how did you manage to get such a good dinner?"

"We owe it to my mother, so to her be the praise."

"You have told her, then, what we are going to do?"

"No, not I, for I know nothing about it; but I told her you were coming to see me, and at the same time I gave her the ten sequins."

"And what did your mother say?"

"She said she wouldn't be sorry if you were to love me as you loved my sister."

"I love you better, though I love her well."

"You love her? Why have you left her, then?"

"I have not left her, for we supped together yesterday evening; but we no longer live together as lovers, that is all. I have yielded her up to a rich friend of mine, who has made her fortune."

"That is well, though I don't understand much about these affairs. I hope you will tell Tonine that I have taken her place, and I should be very pleased if you would let her know that you are quite sure you are my first lover."

"And supposing the news vexes her?"

"So much the better. Will you do it for me? it's the first favour I have asked of you."

"I promise to do so."

After this rapid dialogue we took breakfast, and then, perfectly agreed, we went to bed, rather as if we were about to sacrifice to Hymen than to love.

The game was new to Barberine, and her transports, her green notions—which she told me openly—her inexperience, or rather her awkwardness, enchanted me. I seemed for the first time to pluck the fruit of the tree of knowledge, and never had I tasted fruit so delicious. My little maid would have been ashamed to let me see how the first thorn hurt her, and to convince me that she only smelt the rose, she

GIACOMO CASANOVA

strove to make me think she experienced more pleasure than is possible in a first trial, always more or less painful. She was not yet a big girl, the roses on her swelling breasts were as yet but buds, and she was a woman only in her heart.

After more than one assault delivered and sustained with spirit, we got up for dinner, and after we had refreshed ourselves we mounted once more the altar of love, where we remained till the evening. Laura found us dressed and well pleased with each other on her return. I made Barberine another present of twenty sequins, I swore to love her always, and went on my way. At the time I certainly meant to keep to my oath, but that which destiny had in store for me could not be reconciled with these promises which welled forth from my soul in a moment of excitement.

The next morning Righelini took me to see the lodging he had spoken to me about. I liked it and took it on the spot, paying the first quarter in advance. The house belonged to a widow with two daughters, the elder of whom had just been blooded. Righelini was her doctor, and had treated her for nine months without success. As he was going to pay her a visit I went in with him, and found myself in the presence of a fine waxen statue. Surprise drew from me these words:

"She is pretty, but the sculptor should give her some colour."

On which the statue smiled in a manner which would have been charming if her lips had but been red.

"Her pallor," said Righelini, "will not astonish you when I tell you she has just been blooded for the hundred and fourth time."

I gave a very natural gesture of surprise.

This fine girl had attained the age of eighteen years without experiencing the monthly relief afforded by nature, the result being that she felt a deathly faintness three or four times a week, and the only relief was to open the vein.

"I want to send her to the country," said the doctor, "where pure and wholesome air, and, above all, more exercise, will do her more good than all the drugs in the world."

After I had been told that my bed should be made ready by the evening, I went away with Righelini, who told me that the only cure for the girl would be a good strong lover.

"But my dear doctor," said I, "can't you make your own prescription?"

"That would be too risky a game, for I might find myself compelled to marry her, and I hate marriage like the devil."

Though I was no better inclined towards marriage than the doctor, I was too near the fire not to get burnt, and the reader will see in the next chapter how I performed the miraculous cure of bringing the colours of health into the cheeks of this pallid beauty.

V

After leaving Dr. Righelini I went to sup with M. de Bragadin, and gave the generous and worthy old man a happy evening. This was always the case; I made him and his two good friends happy whenever I took meals with them.

Leaving them at an early hour, I went to my lodging and was greatly surprised to find my bedroom balcony occupied. A young lady of an exquisite figure rose as soon as she saw me, and gracefully asked me pardon for the liberty she had taken.

"I am," she said, "the statue you saw this morning. We do not light the candles in the evening for fear of attracting the gnats, but when you want to go to bed we will shut the door and go away. I beg to introduce you to my younger sister, my mother has gone to bed."

I answered her to the effect that the balcony was always at her service, and that since it was still early I begged their permission to put on my dressing-gown and to keep them company. Her conversation was charming; she made me spend two most delightful hours, and did not leave me till twelve o'clock. Her younger sister lighted me a candle, and as they went they wished me a good night.

I lay down full of this pretty girl, and I could not believe that she was really ill. She spoke to the point, she was cheerful, clever, and full of spirits. I could not understand how it came to pass that she had not been already cured in a town like Venice, if her cure was really only to be effected in the manner described by Dr. Righelini; for in spite of her pallor she seemed to me quite fair enough to charm a lover, and I believed her to be spirited enough to determine to take the most agreeable medicine a doctor can prescribe.

In the morning I rang the bell as I was getting up, and the younger sister came into my room, and said that as they kept no servant she had come to do what I wanted. I did not care to have a servant when I was not at M. de Bragadin's, as I found myself more at liberty to do what I liked. After she had done me some small services, I asked her how her sister was.

"Very well," said she, "for her pale complexion is not an illness, and she only suffers when her breath fails her. She has a very good appetite, and sleeps as well as I do."

"Whom do I hear playing the violin?"

"It's the dancing master giving my sister a lesson."

I hurried over my dressing that I might see her; and I found her charming, though her old dancing master allowed her to turn in her toes. All that this young and beautiful girl wanted was the Promethean spark, the colour of life; her whiteness was too like snow, and was distressing to look at.

The dancing master begged me to dance a minuet with his pupil, and I assented, asking him to play larghissimo. "The signorina would find it too tiring," said he; but she hastened to answer that she did not feel weak, and would like to dance thus. She danced very well, but when we had done she was obliged to throw herself in a chair. "In future, my dear master," said she, "I will only dance like that, for I think the rapid motion will do me good."

When the master was gone, I told her that her lessons were too short, and that her master was letting her get into bad habits. I then set her feet, her shoulders, and her arms in the proper manner. I taught her how to give her hand gracefully, to bend her knees in time; in fine, I gave her a regular lesson for an hour, and seeing that she was getting rather tired I begged her to sit down, and I went out to pay a visit to M. M.

I found her very sad, for C—— C——'s father was dead, and they had taken her out of the convent to marry her to a lawyer. Before leaving C—— C—— had left a letter for me, in which she said that if I would promise to marry her at some time suitable to myself, she would wait for me, and refuse all other offers. I answered her straightforwardly that I had no property and no prospects, that I left her free, advising her not to refuse any offer which might be to her advantage.

In spite of this dismissal C—— C—— did not marry N—— till after my flight from The Leads, when nobody expected to see me again in Venice. I did not see her for nineteen years, and then I was grieved to find her a widow, and poorly off. If I went to Venice now I should not marry her, for at my age marriage is an absurdity, but I would share with her my little all, and live with her as with a dear sister.

GIACOMO CASANOVA

When I hear women talking about the bad faith and inconstancy of men, and maintaining that when men make promises of eternal constancy they are always deceivers, I confess that they are right, and join in their complaints. Still it cannot be helped, for the promises of lovers are dictated by the heart, and consequently the lamentations of women only make me want to laugh. Alas! we love without heeding reason, and cease to love in the same manner.

About this time I received a letter from the Abbe de Bernis, who wrote also to M—— M——. He told me that I ought to do my utmost to make our nun take a reasonable view of things, dwelling on the risks I should run in carrying her off and bringing her to Paris, where all his influence would be of no avail to obtain for us that safety so indispensable to happiness. I saw M—— M——; we shewed each other our letters, she had some bitter tears, and her grief pierced me to the heart. I still had a great love for her in spite of my daily infidelities, and when I thought of those moments in which I had seen her given over to voluptuousness I could not help pitying her fate as I thought of the days of despair in store for her. But soon after this an event happened which gave rise to some wholesome reflections. One day, when I had come to see her, she said,

"They have just been burying a nun who died of consumption the day before yesterday in the odour of sanctity. She was called 'Maria Concetta.' She knew you, and told C—— C—— your name when you used to come to mass on feast days. C—— C—— begged her to be discreet, but the nun told her that you were a dangerous man, whose presence should be shunned by a young girl. C—— C—— told me all this after the mask of Pierrot."

"What was this saint's name when she was in the world?"

"Martha."

"I know her."

I then told M—— M—— the whole history of my loves with Nanette and Marton, ending with the letter she wrote me, in which she said that she owed me, indirectly, that eternal salvation to which she hoped to attain.

In eight or ten days my conversation with my hostess' daughter— conversation which took place on the balcony, and which generally lasted till midnight—and the lesson I gave her every morning, produced the inevitable and natural results; firstly, that she no longer complained of her breath failing, and, secondly, that I fell in love with her. Nature's cure had not yet relieved her, but she no longer needed to be let blood. Righelini came to visit her as usual, and seeing that she was better he prophesied that nature's remedy, without which only art could keep her alive, would make all right before the autumn. Her mother looked upon me as an angel sent by God to cure her daughter, who for her part shewed me that gratitude which with women is the first step towards love. I had made her dismiss her old dancing master, and I had taught her to dance with extreme grace.

At the end of these ten or twelve days, just as I was going to give her her lesson, her breath failed instantaneously, and she fell back into my arms like a dead woman. I was alarmed, but her mother, who had become accustomed to see her thus, sent for the surgeon, and her sister unlaced her. I was enchanted with her exquisite bosom, which needed no colouring to make it more beautiful. I covered it up, saying that the surgeon would make a false stroke if he were to see her thus uncovered; but feeling that I laid my hand upon her with delight, she gently repulsed me, looking at me with a languishing gaze which made the deepest impression on me.

The surgeon came and bled her in the arm, and almost instantaneously she recovered full consciousness. At most only four ounces of blood were taken from her, and her mother telling me that this was the utmost extent to which she was blooded, I saw it was no such matter for wonder as Righelini represented it, for being blooded twice a week she lost three pounds of blood a month, which she would have done naturally if the vessels had not been obstructed.

The surgeon had hardly gone out of the door when to my astonishment she told me that if I would wait for her a moment she would come back and begin her dancing. This she did, and danced as if there had been nothing the matter.

Her bosom, on which two of my senses were qualified to give evidence, was the last stroke, and made me madly in love with her. I returned to the house in the evening, and found her in her room with the sister. She told me that she was expecting her god-father, who was an intimate friend of her father's, and had come every evening to spend an hour with her for the last eighteen years.

"How old is he?"

"He is over fifty."

"Is he a married man?"

"Yes, his name is Count S——. He is as fond of me as a father would be, and his affection has continued the same since my childhood. Even his wife comes to see me sometimes, and to ask me to dinner. Neat autumn I am going into the country with her, and I hope the fresh air will do me good. My god-father knows you are staying with us and is satisfied. He does not know you, but if you like you can make his acquaintance."

I was glad to hear all this, as I gained a good deal of useful information without having to ask any awkward questions. The friendship of this Greek looked very like love. He was the husband of Countess S——, who had taken me to the convent at Muran two years before.

I found the count a very polite man. He thanked me in a paternal manner for my kindness to his daughter, and begged me to do him the honour of dining with him on the following day, telling me that he would introduce me to his wife. I accepted his invitation with pleasure, for I was fond of dramatic situations, and my meeting with the countess promised to be an exciting one. This invitation bespoke the courteous gentleman, and I charmed my pretty pupil by singing his praises after he had gone.

"My god-father," said she, "is in possession of all the necessary documents for withdrawing from the house of Persico our family fortune, which amounts to forty thousand crowns. A quarter of this sum belongs to me, and my mother has promised my sister and myself to share her dowry between us."

I concluded from this that she would bring her husband fifteen thousand Venetian ducats.

I guessed that she was appealing to me with her fortune, and wished to make me in love with her by shewing herself chary of her favours; for whenever I allowed myself any small liberties, she checked me with words, of remonstrance to which I could find no answer. I determined to make her pursue another course.

Next day I took her with me to her god-father's without telling her that I knew the countess. I fancied the lady would pretend not to know me, but I was wrong, as she welcomed me in the handsomest manner as if I were an old friend. This, no doubt, was a surprise for the count, but he was too much a man of the world to, shew any astonishment. He asked her when she had made my acquaintance, and she, like a woman of experience, answered without the slightest hesitation that we had seen each other two years ago at Mira. The matter was settled, and we spent a very pleasant day.

Towards evening I took the young lady in my gondola back to the house, but wishing to shorten the journey I allowed myself to indulge in a few caresses. I was hurt at being responded to by reproaches, and for that reason, as soon as she had set foot on her own doorstep, instead of getting out I went to Tonine's house, and spent nearly the whole night there with the ambassador, who came a little after me. Next day, as I did not get up till quite late, there was no dancing lesson, and when I excused myself she told me not to trouble any more about it. In the evening I sat on the balcony far into the night, but she did not come. Vexed at this air of indifference I rose early in the morning and went out, not returning till nightfall. She was on the balcony, but as she kept me at a respectful distance I only talked to her on commonplace subjects. In the morning I was roused by a tremendous noise. I got up, and hurriedly putting on my dressing-gown ran into her room to see what was the matter, only to find her dying. I had no need to feign an interest in her, for I felt the most tender concern. As it was at the beginning of July it was extremely hot, and my fair invalid was only covered by a thin sheet. She could only speak to me with her eyes, but though the lids were lowered she looked upon me so lovingly! I asked her if she suffered from palpitations, and laying my hand upon her heart I pressed a fiery kiss upon her breast. This was the electric spark, for she gave a sigh which did her good. She had not strength to repulse the hand which I pressed amorously upon her heart, and becoming bolder I fastened my burning lips upon her languid mouth. I warmed her with my breath, and my audacious hand penetrated to the very sanctuary of bliss. She made an effort to push me back, and told me with her eyes, since she could not speak, how insulted she felt. I drew back my hand, and at that moment the surgeon came. Hardly was the vein opened when she drew a long breath, and by the time the operation was over she wished to get up. I entreated her to stay in bed, and her mother added her voice to mine; at last I persuaded her, telling her that I would not leave her for a second, and that I would have my dinner by her bedside. She then put on a corset and asked her sister to draw a sarcenet coverlet over her, as her limbs could be seen as plainly as through a crape veil.

Having given orders for my dinner, I sat down by her bedside, burning with love, and taking her hand and covering it with kisses I told her that I was sure she would get better if she would let herself love.

"Alas!" she said, "whom shall I love, not knowing whether I shall be loved in return?"

I did not leave this question unanswered, and continuing the amorous discourse with animation I won a sigh and a lovelorn glance. I put my hand on her knee, begging her to let me leave it there, and promising to go no farther, but little by little I attained the center, and strove to give her some pleasant sensations.

"Let me alone," said she, in a sentimental voice, drawing away, "'tis perchance the cause of my illness."

"No, sweetheart," I replied, "that cannot be." And my mouth stopped all her objections upon her lips.

I was enchanted, for I was now in a fair way, and I saw the moment of bliss in the distance, feeling certain that I could effect a cure if the doctor was not mistaken. I spared her all indiscreet questions out of regard for her modesty; but I declared myself her lover, promising to ask nothing of her but what was necessary to feed the fire of my love. They sent me up a very good dinner, and she did justice to it; afterwards saying that she was quite well she got up, and I went away to dress myself for going out. I came back early in the evening, and found her on my balcony. There, as I sat close to her looking into her face, speaking by turns the language of the eyes and that of sighs, fixing my amorous gaze upon those charms which the moonlight rendered sweeter, I made her share in the fire which consumed me; and as I pressed her amorously to my bosom she completed my bliss with such warmth that I could easily see that she thought she was receiving a favour and not granting one. I sacrificed the victim without staining the altar with blood.

Her sister came to tell her that it grew late.

"Do you go to bed," she answered; "the fresh air is doing me good, and I want to enjoy it a little longer."

As soon as we were alone we went to bed together as if we had been doing it for a whole year, and we passed a glorious night, I full of love and the desire of curing her, and she of tender and ardent voluptuousness. At day-break she embraced me, her eyes dewy with bliss, and went to lie down in her own bed. I, like her, stood in need of a rest, and on that day there was no talk of a dancing lesson. In spite of the fierce pleasure of enjoyment and the transports of this delightful girl, I did not for a moment lay prudence aside. We continued to pass such nights as these for three weeks, and I had the pleasure of seeing her thoroughly cured. I should doubtless have married her, if an event had not happened to me towards the end of the month, of which I shall speak lower down.

You will remember, dear reader, about a romance by the Abbe Chiari, a satirical romance which Mr. Murray had given me, and in which I fared badly enough at the author's hands I had small reason to be pleased with him, and I let him know my opinion in such wise that the abbe who dreaded a caning, kept upon his guard. About the same time I received an anonymous letter, the writer of which told me that I should be better occupied in taking care of myself than in thoughts of chastising the abbe, for I was threatened by an imminent danger. Anonymous letter-writers should be held in contempt, but one ought to know how, on occasion, to make the best of advice given in that way. I did nothing, and made a great mistake.

About the same time a man named Manuzzi, a stone setter for his first trade, and also a spy, a vile agent of the State Inquisitors—a man of whom I knew nothing—found a way to make my acquaintance by offering to let me have diamonds on credit, and by this means he got the entry of my house. As he was looking at some books scattered here and there about the room, he stopped short at the manuscripts which were on magic. Enjoying foolishly enough, his look of astonishment, I shewed him the books which teach one how to summon the elementary spirits. My readers will, I hope, do me the favour to believe that I put no faith in these conjuring books, but I had them by me and used to amuse myself with them as one does amuse one's self with the multitudinous follies which proceed from the heads of visionaries. A few days after, the traitor came to see me and told me that a collector, whose name he might not tell me, was ready to give me a thousand sequins for my five books, but that he would like to examine them first to see if they were genuine. As he promised to let me have them back in twenty-four hours, and not thinking much about the matter, I let him have them. He did not fail to bring them back the next day, telling me that the collector thought them forgeries. I found out, some years after, that he had taken them to the State Inquisitors, who thus discovered that I was a notable magician.

Everything that happened throughout this fatal month tended to my ruin, for Madame Memmo, mother of Andre, Bernard, and Laurent Memmo, had taken it into her head that I had inclined her sons to atheistic opinions, and took counsel with the old knight Antony Mocenigo, M. de Bragadin's uncle, who was angry with me, because, as he said, I had conspired to seduce his nephew. The matter was a serious one, and an auto-da-fe was very possible, as it came under the jurisdiction of the Holy Office—a kind of wild beast, with which it is not good to quarrel. Nevertheless, as there would be some difficulty in shutting me up in the ecclesiastical prisons of the Holy Office, it was determined to carry my case before the State Inquisitors, who took upon themselves the provisional duty of putting a watch upon my manner of living.

M. Antony Condulmer, who as a friend of Abbe Chiari's was an enemy of mine, was then an Inquisitor of State, and he took the opportunity of looking upon me in the light of a disturber of the peace of the commonwealth. A secretary of an embassy, whom I knew some years after, told me that a paid informer, with two other witnesses, also, doubtless, in the pay of this grand tribunal, had declared that I was guilty of only believing in the devil, as if this absurd belief, if it were possible, did not necessarily connote a belief in God! These three honest fellows testified with an oath that when I lost money at play, on which occasion all the faithful are wont to blaspheme, I was never heard to curse the devil. I was further accused of eating meat all the year round, of only going to hear fine masses, and I was vehemently suspected of being a Freemason. It was added that I frequented the society of foreign ministers, and that living as I did with three noblemen, it was certain that I revealed, for the large sums which I was seen to lose, as many state secrets as I could worm out of them.

All these accusations, none of which had any foundation in fact, served the Tribunal as a pretext to treat me as an enemy of the commonwealth and as a prime conspirator. For several weeks I was counselled by persons whom I might have trusted to go abroad whilst the Tribunal was engaged on my case. This should have been enough, for the only people who can live in peace at Venice are those whose existence the Tribunal is ignorant of, but I obstinately despised all these hints. If I had listened to the indirect advice which was given me, I should have become anxious, and I was the sworn foe of all anxiety. I kept saying to myself, "I feel remorse for nothing and I am therefore guilty of nothing, and the innocent have nothing to fear." I was a fool, for I argued as if I had been a free man in a free country. I must also confess that what to a great extent kept me from thinking of possible misfortune was the actual misfortune which oppressed me from morning to night. I lost every day, I owed money everywhere, I had pawned all my jewels, and even my portrait cases, taking the precaution, however, of removing the portraits, which with my important papers and my amorous letters I had placed in the hands of Madame Manzoni. I found myself avoided in society. An old senator told me, one day, that it was known that the young Countess Bonafede had become mad in consequence of the love philtres I had given her. She was still at the asylum, and in her moments of delirium she did nothing but utter my name with curses. I must let my readers into the secret of this small history.

This young Countess Bonafede, to whom I had given some sequins a few days after my return to Venice, thought herself capable of making me continue my visits, from which she had profited largely. Worried by her letters I went to see her several times, and always left her a few sequins, but with the exception of my first visit I was never polite enough to give her any proofs of my affection. My coldness had baulked all her endeavours for a year, when she played a criminal part, of which, though I was never able absolutely to convict her, I had every reason to believe her guilty.

She wrote me a letter, in which she importuned me to come and see her at a certain hour on important business.

My curiosity, as well as a desire to be of service to her, took me there at the appointed time; but as soon as she saw me she flung her arms round my neck, and told me that the important business was love. This made me laugh heartily, and I was pleased to find her looking neater than usual, which, doubtless, made me find her looking prettier. She reminded me of St. Andre, and succeeded so well in her efforts that I was on the point of satisfying her desires. I took off my cloak, and asked her if her father were in. She told me he had gone out. Being obliged to go out for a minute, in coming back I mistook the door, and I found myself in the next room, where I was much astonished to see the count and two villainous-looking fellows with him.

"My dear count," I said, "your daughter has just told me that you were out."

"I myself told her to do so, as I have some business with these gentlemen, which, however, can wait for another day."

I would have gone, but he stopped me, and having dismissed the two men he told me that he was delighted to see me, and forthwith began the tale of his troubles, which were of more than one kind. The State Inquisitors had stopped his slender pension, and he was on the eve of seeing himself driven out with his family into the streets to beg his bread. He said that he had not been able to pay his landlord anything for three years, but if he could pay only a quarter's rent, he would obtain a respite, or if he persisted in turning him out, he could make a night-flitting of it, and take up his abode somewhere else. As he only wanted twenty ducats, I took out six sequins and gave them to him. He embraced me, and shed tears of joy; then, taking his poor cloak, he called his daughter, told her to keep me company, and went out.

Alone with the countess, I examined the door of communication between the two rooms and found it slightly open.

"Your father," I said, "would have surprised me, and it is easy to guess what he would have done with the two sbirri who were with him. The plot is clear, and I have only escaped from it by the happiest of chances."

She denied, wept, called God to witness, threw herself on her knees; but I turned my head away, and taking my cloak went away without a word. She kept on writing to me, but her letters remained unanswered, and I saw her no more.

It was summer-time, and between the heat, her passions, hunger, and wretchedness, her head was turned, and she became so mad that she went out of the house stark naked, and ran up and down St. Peter's Place, asking those who stopped her to take her to my house. This sad story went all over the town and caused me a great deal of annoyance. The poor wretch was sent to an asylum, and did not recover her reason for five years. When she came out she found herself reduced to beg her bread in the streets, like all her brothers, except one, whom I found a cadet in the guards of the King of Spain twelve years afterwards.

At the time of which I am speaking all this had happened a year ago, but the story was dug up against me, and dressed out in the attire of fiction, and thus formed part of those clouds which were to discharge their thunder upon me to my destruction.

In the July of 1755 the hateful court gave Messer-Grande instructions to secure me, alive or dead. In this furious style all orders for arrests proceeding from the Three were issued, for the least of their commands carried with it the penalty of death.

Three or four days before the Feast of St. James, my patron saint, M——M—— made me a present of several ells of silver lace to trim a sarcenet dress which I was going to wear on the eve of the feast. I went to see her, dressed in my fine suit, and I told her that I should come again on the day following to ask her to lend me some money, as I did not know where to turn to find some. She was still in possession of the five hundred sequins which she had put aside when I had sold her diamonds.

As I was sure of getting the money in the morning I passed the night at play, and I lost the five hundred sequins in advance. At day-break, being in need of a little quiet, I went to the Erberia, a space of ground on the quay of the Grand Canal. Here is held the herb, fruit, and flower market.

People in good society who come to walk in the Erberia at a rather early hour usually say that they come to see the hundreds of boats laden with vegetables, fruit and flowers, which hail from the numerous islands near the town; but everyone knows that they are men and women who have been spending the night in the excesses of Venus or Bacchus, or who have lost all hope at the gaming-table, and come here to breath a purer air and to calm their minds. The fashion of walking in this place shews how the character of a nation changes. The Venetians of old time who made as great a mystery of love as of state affairs, have been replaced by the modern Venetians, whose most prominent characteristic is to make a mystery of nothing. Those who come to the Erberia with women wish to excite the envy of their friends by thus publishing their good fortune. Those who come alone are on the watch for discoveries, or on the look-out for materials to make wives or husbands jealous, the women only come to be seen, glad to let everybody know that they are without any restraint upon their actions. There was certainly no question of smartness there, considering the disordered style of dress worn. The women seemed to have agreed to shew all the signs of disorder imaginable, to give those who saw them something to talk about. As for the men, on whose arms they leaned, their careless and lounging airs were intended to give the idea of a surfeit of pleasure, and to make one think that the disordered appearance of their companions was a sure triumph they had enjoyed. In short it was the correct thing to look tired out, and as if one stood in need of sleep.

This veracious description, reader, will not give you a very high opinion of the morals of my dear fellow citizens; but what object should I have at my age for deceiving? Venice is not at the world's end, but is well enough known to those whose curiosity brings them into Italy; and everyone can see for himself if my pictures are overdrawn.

After walking up and down for half an hour, I came away, and thinking the whole house still a-bed I drew my key out to open the door, but what was my astonishment to find it useless, as the door was open, and what is more, the lock burst off. I ran upstairs, and found them all up, and my landlady uttering bitter lamentations.

"Messer-Grande," she told me, "has entered my house forcibly, accompanied by a band of sbirri. He turned everything upside down, on the pretext that he was in search of a portmanteau full of salt—a highly contraband article. He said he knew that a portmanteau had been landed there the evening before, which was quite true; but it belonged to Count S——, and only contained linen and clothes. Messer-Grande, after inspecting it, went out without saying a word."

He had also paid my room a visit. She told me that she must have some reparation made her, and thinking she was in the right I promised to speak to M. de Bragadin on the matter the same day. Needing rest above all things, I lay down, but my nervous excitement, which I attributed to my heavy losses at play, made me rise after three or four hours, and I went to see M. de Bragadin, to whom I told the whole story begging him to press for some signal amends. I made a lively representation to him of all the grounds on which my landlady required proportionate amends to be made, since the laws guaranteed the peace of all law-abiding people.

I saw that the three friends were greatly saddened by what I said, and the wise old man, quietly but sadly, told me that I should have my answer after dinner.

De la Haye dined with us, but all through the meal, which was a melancholy one, he spoke not a word. His silence should have told me all, if I had not been under the influence of some malevolent genii who would not allow me to exercise my common sense: as to the sorrow of my three friends, I put that down to their friendship for me. My connection with these worthy men had always been the talk of the town, and as all were agreed that it could not be explained on natural grounds, it was deemed to be the effect of some sorcery exercised by me. These three men were thoroughly religious and virtuous citizens; I was nothing if not irreligious, and Venice did not contain a greater libertine. Virtue, it was said, may have compassion on vice, but cannot become its friend.

After dinner M. de Bragadin took me into his closet with his two friends, from whom he had no secrets. He told me with wonderful calmness that instead of meditating vengeance on Messer-Grande I should be thinking of putting myself in a place of safety. "The portmanteau," said he, "was a mere pretext; it was you they wanted and thought to find. Since your good genius has made them miss you, look out for yourself; perhaps by to-morrow it may be too late. I have been a State Inquisitor for eight months, and I know the way in which the arrests ordered by the court are carried out. They would not break open a door to look for a box of salt. Indeed, it is possible that they knew you were out, and sought to warn you to escape in this manner. Take my advice, my dear son, and set out directly for Fusina, and thence as quickly as you can make your way to Florence, where you can remain till I write to you that you may return with safety. If you have no money I will give you a hundred sequins for present expenses. Believe me that prudence bids you go."

Blinded by my folly, I answered him that being guilty of nothing I had nothing to fear, and that consequently, although I knew his advice was good, I could not follow it.

"The high court," said he, "may deem you guilty of crimes real or imaginary; but in any case it will give you no account of the accusations against you. Ask your oracle if you shall follow my advice or not." I refused because I knew the folly of such a proceeding, but by way of excuse I said that I only consulted it when I was in doubt. Finally, I reasoned that if I fled I should be shewing fear, and thus confessing my guilt, for an innocent man, feeling no remorse, cannot reasonably be afraid of anything.

"If secrecy," said I, "is of the essence of the Court, you cannot possibly judge, after my escape, whether I have done so rightly or wrongly. The same reasons, which, according to your excellence, bid me go, would forbid my return. Must I then say good-bye for ever to my country, and all that is dear to me?" As a last resource he tried to persuade me to pass the following day and night, at least, at the palace. I am still ashamed of having refused the worthy old man to whom I owed so much this favour; for the palace of a noble is sacred to the police who dare not cross its threshold without a special order from the Tribunal, which is practically never given; by yielding to his request I should have avoided a grievous misfortune, and spared the worthy old man some acute grief.

I was moved to see M. de Bragadin weeping, and perhaps I might have granted to his tears that which I had obstinately refused to his arguments and entreaties. "For Heaven's sake!" said I, "spare me the harrowing sight of your tears." In an instant he summoned all his strength to his assistance, made some indifferent remarks, and then, with a smile full of good nature, he embraced me, saying, "Perhaps I may be fated never to see you again, but 'Fata viam invenient'."

I embraced him affectionately, and went away, but his prediction was verified, for I never saw him again; he died eleven years afterwards. I found myself in the street without feeling the slightest fear, but I was in a good deal of trouble about my debts. I had not the heart to go to Muran to take away from M. M. her last five hundred sequins, which sum I owed to the man who won it from me in the night; I preferred asking him to wait eight days, and I did so. After performing this unpleasant piece of business I returned home, and, having consoled my landlady to the utmost of my power, I kissed the daughter, and lay down to sleep. The date was July 25th, 1755.

Next morning at day-break who should enter my room but the awful Messer-Grande. To awake, to see him, and to hear him asking if I were Jacques Casanova, was the work of a moment. At my "yes, I am Casanova," he told me to rise, to put on my clothes, to give him all the papers and manuscripts in my possession, and to follow him.

"On whose authority do you order me to do this?"

"By the authority of the Tribunal."

A Note About the Author

Giacomo Casanova (1725–1798) was an Italian adventurer and author. Born in Venice, Casanova was the eldest of six siblings born to Gaetano Casanova and Zanetta Farussi, an actor and actress. Raised in a city noted for its cosmopolitanism, night life, and glamor, Casanova overcame a sickly childhood to excel in school, entering the University of Padua at the age of 12. After graduating in 1742 with a degree in law, he struggled to balance his work as a lawyer and low-level cleric with a growing gambling addiction. As scandals and a prison sentence threatened to derail his career in the church, Casanova managed to find work as a scribe for a powerful Cardinal in Rome, but was soon dismissed and entered military service for the Republic of Venice. Over the next several years, he left the service, succeeded as a professional gambler, and embarked on a Grand Tour of Europe. Towards the end of his life, Casanova worked on his exhaustive, scandalous memoirs, a 12-volume autobiography reflecting on a legendary life of romance and debauchery that brought him from the heights of aristocratic society to the lows of illness and imprisonment. Recognized for his self-styled sensationalism as much as he is for his detailed chronicling of 18th century European culture, Casanova is a man whose name is now synonymous with the kind of life he led—fast, fearless, and free.

A Note from the Publisher

Spanning many genres, from non-fiction essays to literature classics to children's books and lyric poetry, Mint Edition books showcase the master works of our time in a modern new package. The text is freshly typeset, is clean and easy to read, and features a new note about the author in each volume. Many books also include exclusive new introductory material. Every book boasts a striking new cover, which makes it as appropriate for collecting as it is for gift giving. Mint Edition books are only printed when a reader orders them, so natural resources are not wasted. We're proud that our books are never manufactured in excess and exist only in the exact quantity they need to be read and enjoyed.

bookfinity™

Discover more of your favorite classics with Bookfinity™.

- Track your reading with custom book lists.
- Get great book recommendations for your personalized Reader Type.
- Add reviews for your favorite books.
- AND MUCH MORE!

Visit **bookfinity.com** and take the fun Reader Type quiz to get started.

Enjoy our classic and modern companion pairings!

Classic & Modern

www.ingramcontent.com/pod-product-compliance
Lightning Source LLC
Chambersburg PA
CBHW020558030426
42337CB00013B/1134